Beloved Names

of God

Beloved Names

of God

David McLaughlan

BARBOUR
PUBLISHING

Published by Barbour Publishing, Inc., P.O. Box 719, Uhrichsville, Ohio 44683, www.barbourbooks.com

Our mission is to publish and distribute inspirational products offering exceptional value and biblical encouragement to the masses.

Member of the
Evangelical Christian
Publishers Association

Printed in the United States of America.

Introduction

Covering the who, what, where, when, and why
of God's glorious names, *Beloved Names of God* was
designed with ease of use in mind. Pinpointing 99
of His most important names, each entry includes

- a significant scriptural example

- the name's relationship to the Holy Trinity

- the total number of times the name appears
  in scripture

- a brief interpretation of the name's meaning

- a concise explanation of the name's biblical
  origin

- contemporary devotional analysis

If you'd like to know God better, this inspirational
quick reference will help reveal the incredible breadth
of God's personality as depicted in scripture. We hope
that within these pages you will find joy, peace, and
strength for your journey ahead.

THE EDITORS

I Am

And God said unto Moses, I AM THAT I AM:
and he said, Thus shalt thou say unto the children of Israel,
I AM hath sent me unto you.*
EXODUS 3:14 KJV

- Name of God the Father

- "I AM THAT I AM" appears once in the KJV. God also calls Himself "I Am" once.

- In Hebrew, *Ehyeh asher ehyeh* or *Hayah* means "I am that I am" or "I will be that I will be."

- Speaking through the burning bush, God instructed Moses to call Him by the name *I Am* when he announced himself as the chosen leader of the Israelites.

Traveling to ancient cultures is a mind-blowing experience. How amazing it is to walk on roads trod by Roman soldiers; to stand in the same room where Christopher Columbus received his commission to sail to the New World from Isabella and Ferdinand; or to climb up the Areopagus, or Mars Hill, in Athens, where Paul preached to the Greeks. Yet before all cultures existed, before the earth was formed, God was and Jesus was.

When God said that His name was "I Am," He was stating unequivocally that He was the God of Abraham, Isaac, and Jacob and that He would be their

God "from generation to generation" (Exodus 3:15 NIV). God was stating that He never changes. Likewise, Jesus also never changes. The writer of the book of Hebrews declared, "Jesus Christ is the same yesterday and today and forever" (Hebrews 13:8 NIV). And Father and Son are still here, and will be forever. "I AM THAT I AM" has no beginning and no end.

Taken from The Top 100 Names of God
ELLYN SANNA

The Rose of Sharon

I am the rose of Sharon.
SONG OF SOLOMON 2:1 KJV

- Name of God the Son

- The description "the rose of Sharon" appears once in the KJV.

- In biblical times, the Plain of Sharon (to which this name refers) was known for its beauty and majesty. A popular garden variety of hibiscus borrows its name from this passage.

- Though the context of Song of Solomon 2:1 doesn't imply a literal connection to Jesus, many biblical scholars agree that it is a symbolic reference to Jesus' undying and perfect devotion to His children. The loving relationship He desires to establish with us all is revealed through the exchange between Solomon and the Shulamite woman.

Child of God, there is no mood of your life where Jesus fails to fit your need, to brighten as a brilliant rose your life. In joy or sorrow, sunshine or shadow, day or night, He blooms for you. Behold Him, then, today, not only on the cross for you, not only on the throne, but near you, close beside your path, the Rose of Sharon.

Taken from *The Wonderful Names of Our Wonderful Lord*

Ancient of Days

*"As I looked, thrones were set in place,
and the Ancient of Days took his seat.
His clothing was as white as snow;
the hair of his head was white like wool.
His throne was flaming with fire,
and its wheels were all ablaze."*
DANIEL 7:9 NIV

- Name of God the Father

- "Ancient of Days" appears three times in
  the KJV.

- Ancient of Days is variously attributed
  to Adam and Jesus. The Western church
  associates the name with God the Father.

- Daniel had a vision of the end times,
  in which great beasts battled for control
  while the Ancient of Days looked on.

Daniel would have been very aware of the tran-
sience of earthly things. The land of his people
had been devastated, and the faith of his fathers had
all but been wiped from the earth. Almost nothing, in
his experience, was permanent—and he told his mas-
ters this. They should turn to God, who ruled when
their empires were but a dream and would rule still
when their empires turned to dust.

When Adam walked in the Garden, God strolled
beside him. Those were ancient days for Moses, but
God strode the desert with him as well. The days of

10

Moses were ancient for Daniel, but God still shielded him from the flames. Daniel's days were ancient when Jesus became flesh, but God was an adoring Father to Him. Even now, God walks with you; Ancient of Days, and as young as a heart in love.

Vine

I am the true vine, and my Father is the husbandman.
JOHN 15:1 KJV

- Name of God the Son

- Jesus refers to Himself as the "vine" twice in the KJV.

- Vines and vineyards would have been a common sight around Jerusalem in biblical times. In fact, some of the winepresses those vineyards supplied can still be visited.

- The phrase "I am the true vine" comes as Jesus prepares for His death and seeks to prepare His disciples for what will come. He is declaring Himself the fulfillment of Israel's promise, while letting them know that His work will go on through them, the fruits of the Vine.

Grapes can be used to make wine, and wine can change how people see the world!

The grapes wouldn't exist if it wasn't for the vine. The vine would be useless without nutrition from the soil. Likewise, Jesus as the Vine is the direct link between the Father and the fruit of His work, the person of faith.

Drawing strength from the Creator and constantly supported by the Vine, we, too, can change how people see the world!

Holy Ghost

- Name of God the Holy Spirit

- The name "Holy Ghost" appears ninety times in the KJV.

- The term *Holy Ghost* derives from the Old English term *gast* meaning "spirit" or "soul."

- The Holy Ghost or Holy Spirit appears throughout the New Testament, giving the gift of a son to Mary, watching over Jesus' baptism, and empowering the apostles.

In the 1940s Jimmy Wilson was a shepherd looking for his flock in a snowstorm with his dog, Peat. Completely lost and freezing, he stumbled across fresh footprints. Thinking they might lead him to safety, he followed them for a while before realizing they were his own. Feeling cold, tired, and defeated, he turned to his companion, realizing Peat may know the way home better than himself. "Go home, boy!" he commanded, trusting the dog would lead the way. And Peat did head for home, just close enough for Jimmy to follow. They both made it safely back and found the sheep along the way!

Jesus described the Holy Ghost as a "Comforter," a companion who would always be with us, ready to offer guidance. It's often seen as the active force that points us toward the Father and heaven. Just as Jimmy put all his trust in his dog's instincts, we can have faith that relying on the Holy Ghost will lead us down the right path.

Good Shepherd

"I am the good shepherd.
The good shepherd lays down his life for the sheep."
JOHN 10:11 NIV

- Name of God the Son

- Jesus says, "I am the good shepherd" twice in the NIV.

- In calling Himself the "good shepherd," Jesus was fulfilling a prophecy of Isaiah (40:11).

- In John 10 Jesus told the Pharisees that He knows His people and they know Him, and that He would live and die for His flock.

As a boy, the future Olympic athlete and missionary Eric Liddell loved hearing his mother sing about "The Ninety-nine and the One." Eventually she refused to sing it anymore. Why? Because he cried every time she sang it, and she couldn't bear to see him so upset. But Eric pleaded. So she sang about the Shepherd (Jesus Christ), who had brought ninety-nine of His sheep in from the storm—only to go out again, risking His life and searching the dangerous cliffs, all to rescue one little lamb. An ordinary shepherd would have been thankful for the remaining ninety-nine and his own safety. But the Good Shepherd gave His life so that every lost lamb might be saved.

The story goes that Eric Liddell would stand

with his face to the wall, just so his mom would not see him cry over such a wonderful love.

Working as a missionary in China at the start of WWII, he sent his own family to safety then walked, alone, into a land being fought over by five armies. The Lord called him home before the war ended, but along the way Eric Liddell showed God's love to many lost lambs.

Jehovah

*That men may know that thou, whose name alone is JEHOVAH,
art the most high over all the earth.*
PSALM 83:18 KJV

- Name of God the Father

- "Jehovah" is referred to seven times in the
  KJV (including three place names).

- The name *Jehovah* is a translation of
  the tetragrammaton (a word with four
  consonants and no vowels) "YHWH." The
  name may originally have been pronounced
  as *Yahweh.*

- Jehovah is the personal name of God. In
  the Bible it is used adoringly and with great
  honor.

There is no record of Jesus ever using the name
Jehovah—and for good reason. Scholars have suggested that had He uttered that name in the presence
of other Jews, especially the Pharisees and Sadducees,
He would have been subjected to extreme punishment.
As God's Son, Jesus knew when He would be arrested
and He chose His words carefully. Instead of Jehovah,
Jesus emphasized God the Father. As John wrote, "But
as many as received him [Jesus], to them gave he power
to become the sons of God [the Father], even to them
that believe on his name" (John 1:12 KJV).

Have you ever been introduced to someone and

two seconds later forgotten his name? Or, someone talks to you and later you have trouble remembering the gist of the conversation. God, the great Jehovah, isn't like that. He heard every cry of His oppressed people in Egypt. He hears, and remembers, every word of every prayer we utter—and then He responds as only an eternal, compassionate God can. Jehovah's arm is still stretched out to save us.

Taken from *The Top 100 Names of God*
ELLYN SANNA

Bridegroom

Jesus answered, "How can the guests of the bridegroom mourn while he is with them? The time will come when the bridegroom will be taken from them; then they will fast."
MATTHEW 9:15 NIV

- Name of God the Son

- Jesus refers to Himself as, or is referred to as, the "bridegroom" fourteen times in the NIV.

- The prophet Isaiah tells Israel that "as a bridegroom rejoices over his bride, so will your God rejoice over you" (Isaiah 62:5 NIV). Jesus is the fulfillment of this prophecy.

- In Matthew 9:15, Jesus tells the Pharisees that He will not be bound by normal social expectations. He also predicts His own death and the time His disciples will have to cope without Him.

Is there a love in this world as intense as that between a couple about to be married? It is thrilling, constant, full of anticipation, full of promise. What would a bridegroom *not* do for his bride?

In earthly marriages, sadly, the passion fades a little with time. We are, after all, only human. But notice in Matthew 9:15 that Jesus isn't referring to Himself as the husband yet. The time when He and His followers will be joined as one has yet to come. In the book of Revelation, John describes how Jesus will return in glory to claim His bride, the "true" church. Until then we are left to wait in fervent anticipation, cultivating our relationship with our most devoted, attentive suitor. And what can we look forward to after the great wedding feast He has planned for us? An eternal, intimate love that will truly last the test of time.

Potter

But now, O LORD, thou art our father;
we are the clay, and thou our potter;
and we all are the work of thy hand.
ISAIAH 64:8 KJV

- Name of God the Father

- The comparison between God as Creator and the potter as a creator is made several times in the Bible, but God is addressed as the "potter" only once.

- Human potters make useful vessels from the clay of the earth. In creating Adam from the earth, God could be described as the first potter.

- In a vision, Isaiah foresaw times of tribulation for Judah and Jerusalem. Seeing cities destroyed and the people enslaved, Isaiah tells God they deserved it, but also pleads with Him not to punish His people endlessly.

Life is full of change. We try to resist it, but often the greatest, most positive changes come from the most traumatic events; events that, given the choice, we would probably avoid repeating.

In a similar way, we can theorize that the clay on a potter's wheel would probably rather stay in the ground. Instead, it is dug out, processed, shipped, sold, soaked, beaten, stretched, and manipulated on its way to becoming something useful—or perhaps even a work of art.

In our own lives, what we perceive as punishment often isn't. Like clay, the Potter puts us on His wheel of life and forms us according to the true purpose for which we were created. It may be a messy, difficult process, but we can trust our Potter to build us up to our full potential.

Alpha and Omega

I am Alpha and Omega, the beginning and the end,
the first and the last.
REVELATION 22:13 KJV

- Name of God the Son

- Jesus is referred to as "Alpha and Omega" four times in the KJV.

- *Alpha* and *omega* are the first and last letters of the Greek alphabet, the language the earliest-known versions of the New Testament books were written in.

- While in exile on the Isle of Patmos, John had a two-part vision, or revelation, in which Jesus asked him to take a warning to the seven churches and revealed to him the end times. Jesus begins His important message to John with these words: "I am Alpha and Omega."

Jesus isn't shy about proclaiming His divinity in Revelation. As well as being alpha and omega, beginning and end, first and last, He also tells John He is the Almighty, a term unequivocally reserved for God.

Not only was Jesus there when *we* were born and will be there when we die, likewise He was there when the *world* was born, and He will bring it all to a glorious end when He finally calls us home.

Wonderful Counselor

For to us a child is born, to us a son is given,
and the government will be on his shoulders.
And he will be called Wonderful Counselor.
ISAIAH 9:6 NIV

- Name of God the Son

- Jesus is called "Wonderful Counselor" once in the NIV.

- In some translations, a comma separates "Wonderful" and "Counselor." It makes no difference. Someone who is both wonderful and a counselor would surely be a wonderful counselor as well.

- By using the name Wonderful Counselor, the prophet Isaiah was foretelling the birth of Christ, praising His attributes, and predicting His everlasting reign.

When noble leaders come to power, they usually surround themselves with wise counselors. Pharaoh took Joseph's advice and guided Egypt through years of drought. Daniel counseled Nebuchadnezzar on his relationship with God. Esther's cousin, Mordecai, saved Xerxes from an assassination plot. The success of such counselors depended largely on their ability to gain their king's ear.

Now imagine the perfect combination of leadership and wisdom: a leader with such great power that

He doesn't need anyone's advice, because He knows all of creation and everyone in it. No one would have to petition to be heard by Him. He would want to speak with each of us every day. The advice He gives would never be wrong, and the Kingdom He rules would never end.

Sound familiar? Thank the Lord today for being our Wonderful Counselor.

Balm of Gilead

Is there no balm in Gilead?
JEREMIAH 8:22 KJV

- Name of God the Father

- Gilead's "balm" is referred to three times in the KJV.

- The place known as Gilead is a mountainous region in present-day Jordan. The balm that bore its name, a healing compound produced from the *Commiphora gileadensis* tree, was famous across the Middle East in biblical times.

- In Jeremiah 8:22, the prophet was bewailing an idol-worshipping Judah around the time of the Babylonian occupation. If they did not change their ways, he warned, their punishment would be such that they would use up all earthly balms and cry for more. Eventually they would have to turn to God. His healing would be the very real equivalent of the famous balm of Gilead.

As well as being the name of a region, *gilead* also meant a hill or mound where one stood to give a testimony. The balm of the Commiphora tree may have been soothing, but anyone who has ever stood on their own personal "gilead" and proclaimed their love of the Lord to the world will know that produces a comfort and healing far more profound than any herbal medicine.

Lamb of God

*The next day John seeth Jesus coming unto him,
and saith, Behold the Lamb of God,
which taketh away the sin of the world.*
JOHN 1:29 KJV

- Name of God the Son

- The "Lamb of God" is referred to only twice.
  Both references are in the book of John.

- Lambs were habitually sacrificed in burnt
  offerings. In Genesis 22:8, Abraham says,
  "God himself will provide the lamb for the
  burnt offering" (NIV). For God Himself to make
  a sacrifice meant something world changing
  was about to happen.

- When John the Baptist saw Jesus coming to
  be baptized, he proclaimed Him as "the Lamb
  of God" and foreshadowed His destiny as a
  sacrifice for all our sins.

What made Jesus different? Napoleon Bonaparte,
war general and emperor of France, felt confi-
dent enough to venture an opinion.

"Alexander, Caesar, Charlemagne, and I have founded
empires," he wrote, "but on what did we rest the creation of our genius? Upon force. Jesus Christ founded
His empire upon love; and at this hour millions of men
would die for Him."

As God incarnate, Jesus was more powerful than

any king, emperor, or war leader that ever lived. And how did He come into the world? As a sacrifice! As a lamb to be slain so the people He loved would live forever. What emperor has ever given so much to his people or paid such a high price for his gift? In weakness there is strength and in His absolute vulnerability to the evil of this world, the Lamb of God had strength enough to save us all from its power. Forever.

The Rock

He is the Rock, his works are perfect, and all his ways are just.
DEUTERONOMY 32:4 NIV

- Name of God the Father

- The name "the Rock" appears thirteen times in scripture.

- Rocks have always been a symbol of strength and steadfastness. Calling upon God as The Rock is a simple metaphor everyone can understand.

- Knowing he was about to die, Moses wrote The Book of the Law to help guide the "stiff-necked" Israelites. He gathered their leaders together for one last speech and began by proclaiming God as The Rock they should rely on.

In biblical times, rocks would have been guideposts in the desert for generations of travelers and comprised the structure of sturdy homes, tombs, and fortresses. In a time when people often lived nomadic lifestyles (either by choice or by conflict), very few things were permanent; and for this reason, things that withstood the test of time were cherished greatly.

God takes the idea of permanence to the extreme. After all, He existed before the rocks were made and will still be around when they are no more. God is there for anyone to hold on to in tempestuous waters and hide behind in fearsome storms. He is there to build our lives, our families, and our futures upon. As the Gospel writer Matthew pointed out, the foolish person builds their house on changeable foundations (the sand), but the wise person builds their house on The Rock.

King of Israel

Nathanael answered and saith unto him,
Rabbi. . .thou art the King of Israel.
JOHN 1:49 KJV

- Name of God the Son

- Jesus is directly referred to as the "King of Israel" four times.

- Israel has a history of warrior kings. In a time of subjugation by the Romans, many hoped the prophesied Messiah would be a king who would lead them to independence.

- In one of the most straightforward proclamations of faith in scripture, John tells the story of Nathanael, who acknowledged and accepted Jesus within seconds of meeting Him.

As a descendant of King David (some say through both sides of His earthly family), Jesus may well have had a legitimate claim to the throne of Israel. But despite His legitimacy, Jesus wasn't interested in crowns. When Nathanael asked how this stranger (Jesus) knew his name, Jesus explained that He saw Nathanael sitting alone under a fig tree. Immediately Nathanael declares Jesus the Son of God and King of Israel.

A bit of an overreaction, surely! But not if Jesus had been working in Nathanael's heart as he sat pondering under that fig tree. We have no reason for Nathanael's solitude or explanation of what his thoughts might have been, but his instant recognition and understanding of Jesus suggests a prior encounter. Jesus didn't want to rule in Israel, He wanted to rule in Nathaniel's heart. Just as He wants to be King of your heart today.

Carpenter

"Isn't this the carpenter? Isn't this Mary's son and the brother of
James, Joseph, Judas, and Simon? Aren't his sisters here with us?"
And they took offense at him.
MARK 6:3 NIV

- Name of God the Son

- Jesus is referred to as "the carpenter" once
  and as "the carpenter's son" once.

- Jesus' earthly father, Joseph, was a *tekton*,
  which means "carpenter, itinerant craftsman,
  builder, or skilled artisan" in Greek. By any
  interpretation, he was a man who worked
  with his hands, and his son Jesus probably
  learned the same trade.

- In this verse Jesus had been teaching in the
  synagogue. The people listening had a hard
  time reconciling the miracle-working teacher
  with the man whose family they all knew.

God came to live among us! Not as a prince, but as
a carpenter!

He came to be with the "salt of the earth," the
common people. God would, forever after, be in the
day's toil, the frustrations of neighbors, the joys of
family, the fears of the vulnerable, and the desperation
of the poor, because Jesus lived with these people.

Jesus knew them (and through them, knew us) as
only their loved ones could.

Breath of the Almighty

The Spirit of God hath made me,
and the breath of the Almighty hath given me life.
JOB 33:4 KJV

- Name of God the Holy Spirit

- The Holy Spirit is referred to once as the "breath of the Almighty."

- The breath of God is described in the Bible as a giver *and* destroyer of life.

- Elihu called Job out on his claim that he was pure and did not deserve punishment. He said the Breath of the Almighty made them both, but the difference was that Elihu made no claim to purity. Job feels he has a case to put before God about his mistreatment. Elihu thinks this is arrogance and Job should simply trust.

We shouldn't be surprised that the Breath of the Almighty is different from ours.

The Breath of the Almighty breathed into Adam, gave life to dust. It parted the Red Sea. King David declared God's breath could expose the foundations of the earth. But just as God can be both fearsome and compassionate, so can this awesome force be the companion, comforter, and guide that Jesus sent to bring us safely home.

Bread of Life

Then Jesus declared, "I am the bread of life.
Whoever comes to me will never go hungry,
and whoever believes in me will never be thirsty. . . .
I am the bread of life."
JOHN 6:35, 48 NIV

- Name of God the Son

- Jesus referred to Himself as "the bread of life"
  twice.

- Bread was an important staple of the Middle
  Eastern diet, essential for sustaining physical
  life. By declaring Himself the Bread of Life,
  Jesus revealed that He was sustenance for a
  different kind of life.

- After the miracle of the loaves and fishes,
  Jesus told a crowd that God had sent them a
  new kind of bread that would sustain them
  for eternity. Him!

This is a hard teaching," the disciples said. But it's
just as hard to swallow two thousand years later.
In a way, the ordinariness and humanness of Jesus is
part of the problem. Because people think they know
Him, they turn away looking for something more ex-
otic and less familiar.

At this point in His mission, many walked away
from Jesus. They were prepared to hear Him talk,
maybe they hoped to see some of His famous miracles,

but when it came to making the commitment—well, He was just one of them. Not so special after all.

The Twelve, however, stayed. When Jesus asked them if they were sure, Peter replied, "Lord, to whom shall we go? You have the words of eternal life" (John 6:68 NIV). Those who left did so because they thought they knew Him. Those who stayed did so because they really did know Him. And they wanted to partake in the Bread of Life.

Adonai

*But Abram said, "Sovereign LORD, what can you
give me since I remain childless and the one who
will inherit my estate is Eliezer of Damascus?"*
GENESIS 15:2 NIV

- Name of God the Father

- The word *Adonai* doesn't actually appear in
  the Bible. The translation, "Sovereign Lord,"
  appears 296 times.

- *Adonai* is actually a plural or emphatic
  version of *Adon*, meaning "Lord." The
  word *Adonai* is used as a substitute for the
  tetragrammaton "YHWH."

- When Abram heard the word of the Lord
  promising to be his very great reward, it
  is the first time in the Bible that God is
  addressed as Adonai.

So why use the plural term Adonai when the singular, Adon, means "Lord"?

For an earthly example of this we might look to the United Kingdom where the king or queen never refers to themselves as I. As sovereign Queen Elizabeth II uses the royal plural, as in, "We think that would be an excellent idea!" In doing so, she emphasizes the fact that she speaks not only as an individual but also as the nation she represents. It would be nice to think of God speaking for Himself—and for all of Creation (as He surely does).

For God to be known by a name that signifies more than one lord doesn't mean there is more than one God. It means that He is much more than just a lord.

Perhaps it's a way of saying "Lord of lords." Or it may, as scholars think, refer to all the aspects of God: i.e., Father, Son, and Holy Spirit.

Strong Tower

The name of the LORD is a strong tower:
the righteous runneth into it, and is safe.
PROVERBS 18:10 KJV

- Name of God the Father

- God is referred to as a "strong tower" twice in the KJV: once in the book of Psalms and once in the book of Proverbs.

- A strong tower is a defensive, protective place where the innocent might withstand the attacks of their enemies.

- King Solomon, the probable author of Proverbs 18, compared the safety found in the Lord with the illusory sense of security some men find in worldly wealth. He pointed out that their conceited attitude will be the cause of their downfall.

The ancient Irish used to build stone towers near their abbeys. When Viking raiders appeared, the monks and villagers would take themselves and their valuables up a ladder and into the towers through doors twelve feet from the ground. Then they would hoist the ladder up behind them, close the door, and wait for the threat to go away.

Isn't it comforting to know that in a world where evil is still attacking, *that's* the kind of protection God offers the faithful?

Messiah

He first found his own brother Simon, and said to him,
"We have found the Messiah"
(which is translated, the Christ).
JOHN 1:41 NKJV

- Name of God the Son

- The title "Messiah" is used twice in the book of Daniel and twice in the book of John.

- *Messiah* means "Redeemer" or "God's Anointed." The designation "Christ" is a translation of *Messiah*.

- Andrew, who had been a follower of John the Baptist, heard Jesus referred to as the Lamb of God. Then John told his own disciples his time was ending and they should follow Jesus. This was significant enough for Andrew to risk ridicule by telling his hardheaded brother, Peter, that the man was the Messiah.

Andrew and Peter were both fishermen; but while Andrew was in the desert with John the Baptist, his brother Peter was at work, possibly supporting a family and certainly supporting a sick mother-in-law. Two different attitudes. But when Andrew found a man who would change everything for them, the very first person he told was his brother.

Have you told your brothers and sisters of the Good News of the Messiah?

Rabbi

The same came to Jesus by night, and said unto him, Rabbi,
we know that thou art a teacher come from God: for no man can
do these miracles that thou doest, except God be with him.
JOHN 3:2 KJV

- Name of God the Son

- Jesus is called "Rabbi" four times in the KJV.

- The word *Rabbi* is often taken to mean "religious teacher," but it can also be interpreted as "great one" or "master."

- In John 3:2, Nicodemus, a wise Pharisee, has met Jesus for the first time. He wasn't yet ready to declare himself a disciple, but he immediately gave Jesus the respectful title of Rabbi. Nicodemus would speak up for Jesus at His trial and help prepare His body for burial.

To be a teacher is a wonderful thing. But Jesus was the Son of God and the Messiah. The title of Rabbi, or teacher, is surely one of His humbler designations.

However, two centuries after His death, countless books have been written about His life and His teachings.

Why? Because Jesus was, and still is, the greatest teacher the world has ever known.

El-Elyon

The LORD thundered from heaven;
the voice of the Most High resounded.
PSALM 18:13 NIV

- Name of God the Father

- The title "Most High" can be found fifty-nine times in the NIV.

- *El-Elyon* is a term believed to predate the time of Moses and refers to "God the Most High." *El* refers to God; *Elyon* means "raised up."

- In his psalm of praise, David joyfully recounts how he called on God to scatter his enemies, including King Saul. The terrifying result included earthquakes, fire, the Lord thundering from heaven, and chasing David's enemies with bolts of lightning. David said the Most High rescued him in his time of need because "he delighted in me" (Psalm 18:19).

The term *El-Elyon* frustrates scholars. They argue and debate over whether it refers to a created god, a creator, one god of two, a god with multiple attributes, a god who died, or the god who took his place.

Sometimes a little education can be a dangerous thing, leading to desperate confusion over something the youngest child of faith knows and David most certainly knew—that there is, and could only ever be, *one* Most High!

42

Prince of Peace

For unto us a child is born, unto us a son is given. . .
and his name shall be called. . .The Prince of Peace.
ISAIAH 9:6 KJV

- Name of God the Son

- Jesus is referred to as the "Prince of Peace" once in the KJV.

- The name *Prince of Peace* assured God's people that despite dire times, God promised to send a Savior into the world whose reign would be just and refreshing.

- The prophet Isaiah predicted dire times for Judah and Israel. The people had turned from God and their leaders had led them to ruin. Despite all this, he was convinced God had not abandoned them. God would eventually send the Prince of Peace.

The title *Prince of Peace* doesn't sound as intimidating as *Lord of War*, but don't let the gentle nature of the word *peace* fool you. The world has been taken to war in the past, but no one has ever been able to lead the whole world to peace. Jesus has the strength and power to do what no other leader ever has. Now *that's* impressive!

Shiloh

The sceptre shall not depart from Judah,
nor a lawgiver from between his feet, until Shiloh come;
and unto him shall the gathering of the people be.
GENESIS 49:10 KJV

- Name of God the Son

- "Shiloh" appears thirty-three times in the KJV, most often as the place name.

- *Shiloh* means "his gift" or "he who was sent or wished for." In place names it indicates a peaceful resting place.

- When Judah, the son of Jacob, was proclaimed as the greatest of his father's sons, it was said that he would rule until Shiloh (the One who was sent or wished for) arrived. In other words, there would be no one greater until the Messiah came.

Israel must walk in darkness under law, until the years may seem eternity, but Shiloh comes at last, and peace. Has Shiloh come to you? And has the peace that passes understanding, the peace *He* made, entered into your soul? For Shiloh came and conquered every foe that could harass you and stands today offering peace. Have you received it? Begin today and "in every thing by prayer and supplication. . .let your requests be made known unto God" (Philippians 4:6 KJV).

Taken from *The Wonderful Names of Our Wonderful Lord*

Ransom

The Son of man came. . .to give his life a ransom for many.
MARK 10:45 KJV

- Name of God the Son

- Jesus is referred to as "ransom" three times in the New Testament. In the Old Testament, Elihu refers to a Christlike "ransom" (Job 33:24), and in Hosea, God says, "I will ransom them from the power of the grave" (13:14 KJV).

- A ransom is traditionally a price paid by one for the freedom of another.

- James and John asked to sit beside Jesus in heaven. The other disciples were annoyed by this, but Jesus assured them that there would be no hierarchy or position of power to strive for in heaven.

Christ is set forth as the penalty paid for the sins of the world. As we were sinners under the judgment wrath of God, He took our place and paid the penalty and the price of our deliverance with His own blood. Listen to the drops of blood as they fall from hands and feet and wounded side! They voice the words "The ransom price for my sins and for the sins of the whole world." Would that men and women everywhere would believe it and receive it.

Taken from *The Wonderful Names of Our Wonderful Lord*

Consuming Fire

*Wherefore we receiving a kingdom which cannot be moved,
let us have grace, whereby we may serve God acceptably with
reverence and godly fear: for our God is a consuming fire.*
HEBREWS 12:28–29 KJV

- Name of God the Father

- God is referred to as a "consuming fire" three
  times in the KJV.

- A consuming fire will take the whole of
  whatever lies in its path. Like a forest fire, it
  devastates the landscape but leaves behind
  space for new growth.

- The author of the book of Hebrews tells
  his readers that God will shake heaven and
  earth and only that which is unshakable (the
  faithful) will remain. He encourages listeners
  to live graceful lives of service—but also to
  have "reverence and godly fear."

The image of fire often conjures fear—fear of painful
burns, and charred devastation. But God's association with fire is different. While we should have a
healthy fear of God's power, we should also remember
that God always has our best interests in mind. In His
mercy, He destroys the dead, sinful parts of us, leaving
behind new opportunities for growth. Despite the pain
it sometimes entails, we should rejoice that our wise
Father is able to bring out the best in us!

Lord of Hosts

*Yea, many people and strong nations shall come to seek the LORD
of hosts in Jerusalem, and to pray before the LORD.*
ZECHARIAH 8:22 KJV

- Name of God the Father

- God is referred to as "Lord of hosts" 243
  times in the KJV.

- *Lord of Hosts* is often taken to mean
  "commander of the armies of heaven."
  However, the phrase *hosts of heaven* is
  sometimes taken to mean everything—
  down to the lowliest creature.

- God proclaimed through Zechariah that
  through Jerusalem's rebirth, He would speak
  to (or conquer) all nations and they would
  come to worship Him there.

Time and again, we read in the Bible of battle lines
drawn and armies facing off, with God directing
the endgame for Israel or Judah. But what about the
private battles we wage, the ones confined to the four
walls of our lives? As believers, we're privileged to have
God, the Lord of Hosts, on our side. Through the Holy
Spirit, He can give us the words to say to assuage a
heated or sticky situation.

Taken from *The Top 100 Names of God*
ELLYN SANNA

Amen

- Name of God the Son

- Jesus is referred to as the "Amen" twice in Revelation.

- *Amen* is usually the conclusion to most Judeo-Christian prayers. It translates from the original Hebrew as "verily" or "truly."

- John was reciting Jesus' warning to the church in Laodicea that He was disappointed by the lack of enthusiasm in their faith. He would prefer they were either "hot or cold."

Laodicea was suffering from lukewarm faith. Laodicea, a thriving metropolis in Asia Minor, a cultural and educational center, was not suffering from plague or drought. No, its condition was much more serious.

Turning the mirror onto this twenty-first century, the parallels between Laodicea and our society are obvious. What Jesus said to the Laodiceans stands today: The Amen (our trustworthy God) is waiting for you to answer His call.

Taken from *The Top 100 Names of God*
ELLYN SANNA

Spirit of Adoption

For ye have not received the spirit of bondage again to fear;
but ye have received the Spirit of adoption,
whereby we cry, Abba, Father.
ROMANS 8:15 KJV

- Name of God the Holy Spirit

- The Holy Spirit is referred to as the "Spirit of adoption" once in the KJV.

- *Adoption* means to accept something or someone and make it your own.

- In Romans 8:15, Paul was describing to the Roman Christians how they were in a new relationship—not one of bondage but one of love to and from the Father.

God doesn't force anyone into a relationship. He will try and try again to kindle trust and acceptance within us, and even when we have walked away countless times, He will still be loving us and eagerly awaiting for us to embrace Him. That acceptance is adoption. Through it God fully accepts us as family and we fully accept Him as our Father.

Star out of Jacob

I shall see him, but not now: I shall behold him, but not nigh:
there shall come a Star out of Jacob, and a Sceptre shall rise
out of Israel, and shall smite the corners of Moab,
and destroy all the children of Sheth.
NUMBERS 24:17 KJV

- Name of God the Son

- Jesus is referred to as the "Star out of Jacob" once in the KJV.

- The Star out of Jacob symbolizes a descendant of Jacob who will outshine all the rest.

- Speaking under the influence of the Holy Spirit, Balaam tells King Balak he has had his eyes opened by God, and he can now see what will ultimately come from the Israelites—the people the king now opposes.

I shall behold him, but not nigh" (Numbers 24:17 KJV). Balaam lived about seven hundred years before Christ, but he knew he would see the Messiah— just not in his lifetime.

Many people believed that the Lord was coming long before He actually arrived. Some suffered and died for that belief. Now *that* is real faith!

How much stronger should our faith be, knowing that these ancient prophecies came true? We know Jesus arrived—and one day He will return!

Abba

And he said, Abba, Father, all things are possible unto thee;
take away this cup from me: nevertheless not what
I will, but what thou wilt.
MARK 14:36 KJV

- Name of God the Father

- God is referred to as "Abba" three times in the KJV.

- *Abba*, in Aramaic, is the familiar version of "Father," the equivalent to the modern "Daddy."

- Jesus was facing His imminent crucifixion and in possibly His most intimate conversation with God, He asked if there was any way He might avoid His fate—before submitting His will completely.

In the early New Testament books, God is the mighty Creator, addressed with reverence, awe, and more than a little fear. And in the time just before Jesus, the title of Abba, or Father, came into popular use, implying a more familiar, loving relationship.

Jesus is the bridge between the older, more formal relationship between man and God and the closer, one-to-one relationship we now have with Him. In Mark 14:36, Jesus addresses God in the most familiar of terms, like a scared child asking his daddy for help. God remained silent and watched as His Son was taken away to His trial and execution. Callous? Hard-hearted? Or weeping silently? No longer Jehovah "the smiter," we now recognize God as a generous Father who suffered for our sake.

Rain upon Mown Grass

He shall come down like rain upon the mown grass.
PSALM 72:6 KJV

- Name of God the Son

- Jesus is referred to as "rain upon the mown grass" once in the KJV.

- *Rain upon mown grass* is an allusion to a natural, life-giving event, as well as the cycle of life, death, and rebirth.

- King David, the probable writer of this psalm, was advanced in age as he wrote. He recalled the times God has visited trials on him but rejoiced in the fact that God always raised him up again. In this psalm, he referred to a King who would come and bless the earth like life-restoring rain, bringing on a time of peace and abundance for the righteous.

Our lives are like grass. We grow and are cut down in season. But there is something in us that need not die with our bodies. Just as the fallen stalks aren't the entirety of the grass, so our bodies are not all there is to us. Through His sacrifice on the cross Jesus became the gentle rain that, after our bodies have succumbed to the "mower," brings us back to a more lush, vibrant life.

The Branch

Hear now, O Joshua the high priest, thou,
and thy fellows that sit before thee:
for they are men wondered at: for, behold,
I will bring forth my servant the BRANCH.
ZECHARIAH 3:8 KJV

- Name of God the Son

- "The Branch" appears six times in the KJV.

- Jesus is a branch—as in the most important branch of the family tree of King David.

- In Zechariah's vision, Joshua (the successor to Moses) is standing in front of God having his earthly clothes replaced by heavenly robes and God introduces him to Jesus.

In a park built on the grounds of what was once an imposing Scottish castle, a tree fell down. The gardeners came along and cut off most of the branches. But wise men that they were, they realised that a few of the tree's roots were still in the ground, and one new branch with fresh green leaves had sprouted since the tree had fallen. They left that little branch, and it grew while the trunk decomposed.

As it reached for the sky, the little branch began to look more and more like a tree in its own right. Eventually roots began to appear from the sides of the trunk, and from the nourishment provided by its fallen parent, a new tree came to be. Now birds live in it, children climb it, and families picnic in its shade.

The lineage of Jesus as recorded in the Bible might be seen as a tree—a family tree.

Adam, Abraham, David, and the others all fell eventually, but from their "trunk" grew a branch that became more than just a branch. And in His shelter we can all rest.

Friend of Sinners

Behold. . .a friend of publicans and sinners.
MATTHEW 11:19 KJV

- Name of God the Son

- Jesus is referred to as a "friend of sinners" twice in the KJV.

- Jesus associated with tax collectors and prostitutes whom polite Jewish society shunned.

- In Matthew 11:19, Jesus was pointing out that just as John the Baptist was not fully appreciated because of his unusual lifestyle, neither was He fully appreciated because of the imperfect nature of the people He associated with.

Jesus contrasted His lifestyle with John the Baptist's and ended by saying, "But wisdom is justified of her children" (Matthew 11:19 KJV).

John and Jesus were the children of wisdom. Their styles didn't matter, their works were the important thing. In John's case, it was to prepare the way. In Jesus' case, it was to come from God straight to those in the greatest need: the publicans and sinners.

Jesus was prepared to put up with scorn, ridicule, and death to be a Friend of Sinners. Let us be "children of wisdom" as well and be wise enough to say, "Lord, I am a sinner. Be my friend."

God of All Comfort

*Blessed be God, even the Father of our Lord Jesus Christ,
the Father of mercies, and the God of all comfort.*
2 CORINTHIANS 1:3 KJV

- Name of God the Father

- God is referred to as the "God of all comfort"
  once in the KJV.

- The name *God of All Comfort* implies that God
  is the source from which all good things flow.

- In 2 Corinthians 1, Paul was writing to the
  church in Corinth. He begins by introducing
  himself as "an apostle of Jesus Christ by the
  will of God" and then goes on to bless them
  in the name of the Father of mercies and the
  "God of all comfort."

No doubt the young father thought he was shar-
ing the load when he and his family went swim-
ming in the hotel pool. While his wife took their baby
into the changing room, he took his two-year-old son
with him. He did a good job putting the child's needs
first, and he spoke in soothing tones. But despite telling
him how much fun it was going to be in the pool, the
little boy cried for his mother the whole time. His sobs
were heartbreaking. In reality, the mother wouldn't have
done anything differently from the father, but her mere
presence was a comfort to the child.

We have a similar relationship with God. Without

Him, we are desolate and no one can take His place.

The young family did have a good time splashing in the pool. Harmony was restored once the little boy was reunited with his source of all comfort.

Passover Lamb

Get rid of the old yeast, so that you may be
a new unleavened batch—as you really are.
For Christ, our Passover lamb, has been sacrificed.
1 CORINTHIANS 5:7 NIV

- Name of God the Son

- Jesus is referred to as the "Passover lamb"
  once in the NIV.

- The blood of a lamb was used to mark the
  doors of Jewish households so they might be
  spared on the night God began the plagues
  of Egypt. This ritual is now celebrated as the
  feast of Passover.

- In 1 Cornithians 5, Paul wrote to the
  Corinthians demanding that they deal with
  a case of immorality in their community,
  reminding them that Jesus died so they
  might be born anew. The "yeast" he spoke of
  referred to the earthly things that distract us
  from our true spiritual nature.

The original Passover lamb was to be male and
without defect. Its death and blood marked the
Hebrews and spared them from the plagues God visited on Egypt. The sacrifice of the lamb began the
process by which the Jews, as a nation, were reborn—
from slavery in Egypt to free people on their way to the
Promised Land.

Jesus was without defect and His blood marked the possibility of rebirth for each of us. In his letter to the Corinthians, Paul reminded them, and through them us, that because of the sacrifice of God's very own Passover Lamb, Jesus Christ, humankind can be born again, free from the slavery of sin, and on our way to a heavenly home.

Diadem of Beauty

In that day shall the LORD of hosts be for. . .
a diadem of beauty, unto the residue of his people.
ISAIAH 28:5 KJV

- Name of God the Father

- God is referred to as a "diadem of beauty" once in the KJV.

- A diadem is usually taken to mean a crown, but might also be translated as "a jeweled metal band worn around the head." It might also refer to a halo effect around one's head.

- Isaiah was warning the people of Ephraim not to invest all their faith in their own achievement. No matter how impressive they thought they were, their greatest achievements were flawed and would be swept away in time by God's perfection.

Isaiah tells the people of Ephraim not to be too full of themselves (or their own wine). To God should go the praise for their prosperity. He is the Diadem of Beauty, and later Isaiah says the faithful shall be "a crown of glory" and a "royal diadem" (Isaiah 62:3 KJV).

So that's how to sparkle! In living lives of adoration, we become jewels (tiny but nonetheless valuable) on the Diadem of Beauty that is our Maker.

Jehovahjireh

And Abraham called the name of that place Jehovahjireh:
as it is said to this day, In the mount of the LORD it shall be seen.
GENESIS 22:14 KJV

- Name of God the Father

- The name *"Jehovahjireh"* appears once in the
  KJV.

- *Jehovahjireh* means "the Lord shall see."
  At the time, it was simply the name of a
  hill in the land of Moriah. This was the hill
  on which Solomon would later build his
  temple. It is now known as Temple Mount in
  Jerusalem.

- Abraham named the hilltop Jehovahjirah after
  he was asked to sacrifice Isaac, his only son,
  there. With a leaden heart, Abraham prepared
  to do as he was bid. Seeing his faith, the Lord
  stayed Abraham's hand and provided a ram
  as a substitute sacrifice.

Frequently on the news we see a political leader
make an announcement, followed by the ubiqui-
tous "Q and A" session, often cut short by a press secre-
tary. Yet, reflecting on God's request of Abraham, and
Abraham's obedience, it is significant that Abraham
asked no questions. All we read is Abraham's unques-
tioning trust in God, from the beginning of the journey
to Moriah to the provision of the ram, the intended

sacrifice. Abraham believed that Jehovahjireh would provide—and He did.

Taken from *The Top 100 Names of God*
ELLYN SANNA

Chief Cornerstone

Now therefore ye are no more strangers and foreigners,
but fellowcitizens with the saints, and of the household of God;
and are built upon the foundation of the apostles and prophets,
Jesus Christ himself being the chief corner stone.
EPHESIANS 2:19–20 KJV

- Name of God the Son

- Jesus is referred to as the "chief corner stone" twice in the KJV.

- The cornerstone was traditionally the first stone laid in any new building and was associated with sacrifices and prayers for stability and prosperity.

- Paul told the Gentiles (through the Ephesians) that in Christ's death the Jews and Gentiles were brought together as one body.

When bricklayers raise a building up above its foundation, they generally start with the corners. Only when the corners are several rows high do they start building up the walls in between. The walls, being at right angles and all on the same level, then help support each other.

In creating what came to be the modern church, Paul, the Jewish apostle to the Gentiles, brought together Christians from both the Jewish and Gentile worlds. Often separated by thousands of miles and brought up in very different cultures, these people needed something special to bind them together. What Paul needed was a cornerstone—something every man and woman, no matter what their ethnic heritage, could have in common. Something that would support them all.

Of course, he already knew what that was. In Jesus, Paul had found a cornerstone not only big enough to build the church on, but big enough to rest the whole world on.

Light of the World

*Then spake Jesus again unto them, saying, I am the light
of the world: he that followeth me shall not walk in darkness,
but shall have the light of life.*
JOHN 8:12 KJV

- Name of God the Son

- Jesus is referred to as the "light of the world" three times in the KJV.

- The term *light* is used many different ways in the Bible, often referring to "wisdom" or "truth." But we might go straight to the apostle John who declared that "God is light" (1 John 1:5). In this way, Jesus, as the Light of the World, can truly be seen as God in the world.

- John 8:12 recounts the moment when Jesus encountered the woman taken in adultery— and set her free from sin!

The birth of Jesus was God's way of restoring a relationship that had been damaged by the Fall. He was shining a light into our spiritual darkness. Jesus said, "As long as I am in the world, I am the light of the world" John 9:5 KJV). But after He physically left this world, the light did not go out. And it won't! By having Jesus in our hearts, each of us becomes a candle bearer, ensuring the Light still shines for all the world to see.

Physician

*But their scribes and Pharisees murmured against his disciples,
saying, Why do ye eat and drink with publicans and sinners?
And Jesus answering said unto them, They that are whole
need not a physician; but they that are sick.*
LUKE 5:30–31 KJV

- Name of God the Son

- There are four instances of Jesus being
  compared to a physician in the KJV.

- The term *physician* can be applied to a doctor
  or a healer.

- Matthew had invited Jesus to dine with his
  friends. The Pharisees didn't think Matthew's
  friends were the kind of people a respectable
  rabbi should be hanging out with. Jesus told
  them these were *exactly* the people He had
  come to see.

Humans have a great propensity for love and self-sacrifice; we can be generous and understanding;
we are intelligent and can see only too well the benefits
of cooperation; and we know deep down that love is
the answer to every problem. We are capable of a great
deal of devotion and kindness—but our capabilities
don't always translate into action.

Why is it that despite knowing how we ought to
be, and can be, we still allow greed and fear to drag us
down and make us less?

There is no other explanation for this disparity than that we must be sick. Greed was the gift of the serpent in the Garden of Eden. This was the "virus" he infected us all with. Fear is just one of its side effects. Humankind has been sick since the Fall. But there is a solution. Jesus is both the Physician and the medicine that will restore us back to perfect health.

High Priest

Wherefore, holy brethren, partakers of the heavenly calling,
consider the Apostle and High Priest of our profession, Christ Jesus.
HEBREWS 3:1 KJV

- Name of God the Son

- Jesus is referred to as the "High Priest" ten times in the KJV.

- *High priest* refers to the executed founder and very present help of the new Christian movement.

- The speaker in Hebrews 3:1 is reminding his listeners of Jesus' faithfulness to God and their commitment to be faithful to Jesus. He is both the apostle (guided by God) and the high priest (a great teacher sent directly from heaven).

The book of Hebrews is a call to faith and steadfastness in the face of adversity. Those early Christians faced fear and uncertainty, and some of them may have left the church as a result. It's a situation modern Christians know only too well, which is why the message of Hebrews is still applicable to our lives today. Jesus was faithful unto death and beyond; the least we can do is be faithful in life.

Fountain of Living Waters

For my people have committed two evils;
they have forsaken me the fountain of living waters,
and hewed them out cisterns, broken cisterns,
that can hold no water.
JEREMIAH 2:13 KJV

- Name of God the Father

- God is referred to as the "fountain of living waters" twice in the KJV.

- If anyone doubted that one flowed from the other, God describes Himself here as "the fountain of living waters." In the book of John, Jesus tells the Samaritan woman that He is the One from whom she can drink living water (4:10).

- Through Jeremiah, God vents His frustration and amazement that His people have, even after a history of disastrous consequences, once again turned to false gods.

Imagine God's frustration when people started turning to man-made gods and idols—*again*! Everything man-made fails. Even the water-collecting cisterns, hewn from solid rock, would occasionally crack.

Jesus and the Holy Spirit are life-sustaining "waters" that need no cisterns. God is the fountain from which those waters flow. None of them are man-made!

Living Stone

To whom coming, as unto a living stone, disallowed indeed of men,
but chosen of God, and precious.
1 PETER 2:4 KJV

- Name of God the Son

- Jesus is referred to as a "living stone" twice in the KJV.

- The *living stone* is a reference to the fulfillment of the prophecy which talked about the arrival of the Chief Cornerstone.

- Peter was encouraging Christians not to be distracted by the ways of the world but to cling instead to "the Word." Just as people in previous times had God's promise that He would send them a "precious cornerstone" (Isaiah 28:16 NIV), so the people of Peter's time had seen this stone arrive and live! They also saw Him live, die—and live again!

With the Cornerstone of Jesus in place, Peter encouraged those who heard his message—both then and now—to play their parts in the spiritual building that rises from that wonderful foundation. Ancient Sparta boasted that it needed no city walls; each of its soldiers was a brick in its defenses. In much the same way, you and I get to join the Living Stone as building blocks in His lively and living church.

Eternal Spirit

How much more shall the blood of Christ, who through the eternal Spirit offered himself without spot to God, purge your conscience from dead works to serve the living God?
HEBREWS 9:14 KJV

- Name of God the Holy Spirit

- The "eternal Spirit" is referred to once in the KJV.

- The name *Eternal Spirit* refers to the eternal relationship between God the Father, God the Son, and God the Holy Spirit.

- The writer of Hebrews told his listeners that the temples of old and their rituals had been superseded by Christ. It was time to put the old ways aside, as if they had been washed away by the spotless blood of Christ, and move ahead in the guidance of the Holy Spirit.

We all like to say, 'Thank God,'" an atheist commentator once said. "It's only natural." But he didn't explain why it was "only natural" to thank a nonexistent God.

People have placed their faith in strange things: trees, other planets, volcanoes, and even cats! Why? Because we *have* always felt the need to thank someone! It has always been the Eternal Spirit.

The Way

*"I am the way and the truth and the life.
No one comes to the Father except through me."*
JOHN 14:6 NIV

- Name of God the Son

- Jesus calls Himself "the way" once in the NIV.

- *The Way* translates from a Hebrew word
  meaning "road" or "highway."

- Jesus told His disciples He was going to
  His Father's house to prepare places for
  them, and they knew how to find Him if they
  wanted to. Thomas (who was a man of many
  questions) asked how they would know the
  way. Jesus told him they were looking at
  The Way.

If you fly to Rome, London, Buenos Aires, and Dallas, each journey will be similar. They all involve cabs, check-ins, security checks, in-flight snacks, crabby passengers, etc. However, it's when you finally step off the airplane at your particular destinations that you find yourself immersed in completely different landscapes and cultures.

These days, a lot of religions have become homogenized. That is, you can get the same kinds of values and beliefs from many different sources. Just as your flights around the world are virtually one in the same, so it seems with most faiths. Lots of faiths promise a vision of eternal paradise, but there are major differences in the final destinations.

Jesus is your ticket to heaven. He doesn't sell it. He gives it away. You just have to ask. Make sure you know which destination you want. . .then follow The Way.

Seed of the Woman

And I will put enmity between thee and the woman,
and between thy seed and her seed; it shall bruise thy head,
and thou shalt bruise his heel.
GENESIS 3:15 KJV

- Name of God the Son

- Jesus is obliquely prophesized as the Seed
  of the Woman; in other words, a descendant
  of Eve.

- The Seed of the Woman is the descendant of
  Eve (Jesus) who would fulfill the promises
  God made in Eden.

- After the Fall, God told Adam and Eve of the
  trials that lay ahead of them. Adam would
  toil away at the earth, and Eve would bear
  children in pain. Then, turning to the serpent,
  He foretold the ultimate defeat of evil.

These days, tracing your immediate family tree is
pretty easy, but many of us would struggle to trace
our ancestry back to Eden! Matthew describes Jesus'
earthly lineage back as far as Abraham, and Genesis
picks up from there, tracing Abraham to Shem (son of
Noah) and Noah's descendants back to Adam and Eve.

Of course Jesus' other family tree is much simpler.
There's God, the Holy Spirit, Jesus—and that's it!

Emmanuel

Behold, a virgin. . .shall bring forth a son,
and they shall call his name Emmanuel.
MATTHEW 1:23 KJV

- Name of God the Son

- Jesus is referred to as "Emmanuel" once in the KJV.

- *Emmanuel* is a theophoric name—in other words, a name containing the name of God. *El* refers to God and *Immanu* means "with us."

- Joseph, a descendant of David and an honorable man, was "espoused" to Mary, but the marriage had not yet been consummated when she was impregnated by the Holy Ghost. Joseph, not knowing of the divine plan, was considering sending her away to avoid shame on both sides when an angel explained the true nature of the Child.

Mary's pregnancy must have brought images of financial ruin to Joseph's mind! The disgrace would surely cost him customers and his good name. But once the angel explained that God would be living in his house, Joseph stepped up and played a heroic role.

The name Emmanuel and the reassurance that God actually is with us is the greatest comfort we could ever be given. If God is with us, it doesn't matter who is against us!

Restorer

He restoreth my soul: he leadeth me in the
paths of righteousness for his name's sake.
PSALM 23:3 KJV

- Name of God the Father

- The name "Restorer" is mentioned seven
  times in the KJV.

- *Restore* means "make things good as new."

- Psalm 23:3 is part of one of the most famous
  pieces of scripture ever. Believed to have
  been written by King David, the psalm begins,
  "The LORD is my shepherd;" a tribute from a
  king who cared for sheep in his youth. The
  line, "Yea, though I walk through the valley
  of the shadow of death," is often taken as a
  description of Jesus' path to eternal life.

Imagine how amazing it must have been, walking
in the perfect environment of Eden with God right
there by your side! Mankind has become so trapped
by its illusion of independence that such a relationship
has been reduced to a myth—or at best, an impossible
dream.

But it's not impossible. The history of man's inter-
action with God has been one of mutual intimacy. We
can get back to that if we trust in the Restorer!

Dwelling Place

Lord, thou hast been our dwelling place in all generations.
PSALM 90:1 KJV

- Name of God the Father

- God is referred to as a "dwelling place" once in the KJV.

- The psalm writer uses the term *dwelling place* to signify the place where humankind truly belongs.

- Psalm 90 paints a picture of mankind turned loose to vent its youthful (and destructive) nature and suffer from the disapproval of God. But from the beginning, God has always welcomed us back to Him. In our few fleeting years on earth, we should try to acquire wisdom and an appreciation of the Lord before returning, like wayward children, to our final Dwelling Place—our loving, patient Father!

What are houses made of? Timber? Brick? Concrete? Corrugated iron? Leaves and branches? Man may have processed them, but God made them all!

Since the days of Adam and Eve, we have called our physical man-made structures home, but our souls have always been most at home with God. Only when we lay aside the shelter of our divinely inspired bodies will we really know what it is like to be home—in a Dwelling Place we need never leave again!

Majesty on High

Who being the brightness of his glory. . .when he had by himself
purged our sins, sat down on the right hand of the Majesty on high.
HEBREWS 1:3 KJV

- Name of God the Father

- God is referred to as the "Majesty on high" once in the KJV.

- *Majesty* is defined as "grandeur, regal bearing, imposing character, having greatness or supreme authority." Kings and queens have traditionally been referred to as "Your Majesty."

- The writer of Hebrews describes how God used to speak to mankind through prophets, but in later years He spoke to the world through the person of Jesus Christ. And now Jesus has been raised up to sit at the right hand of the Majesty on High.

The term *Your Majesty* has been applied to some doubtful characters. Frederick William of Prussia marched his soldiers through his bedroom, and Queen Juana of Castile had such a jealous streak that she even kept pretty women away from her dead husband's coffin. Nebuchadnezzar from the book of Daniel ate grass!

Of course, there have been good, civilized kings and queens, too, but if we want real majesty, we need to look higher. The throne of heaven is where we will find the true, unflawed Majesty on High.

Author and Finisher of Our Faith

Looking unto Jesus the author and finisher of our faith;
who for the joy that was set before him endured the cross, despising the
shame, and is set down at the right hand of the throne of God.
HEBREWS 12:2 KJV

- Name of God the Son

- Jesus is referred to as the "author and finisher of our faith" once in the KJV.

- As Author and Finisher, Jesus is the creator, fulfiller, and the very last word on Christianity.

- The author of Hebrews urged his listeners to be good examples because many were watching them. He urged them to turn from temptation, knowing that the prize waiting for them was an eternity in heaven in the company of a faithful Savior.

Jesus Christ came telling parables, or stories. Like most stories, they had beginnings, middles, and ends—but they often left people feeling unsatisfied and confused. Likewise, his life was the story of the creation of Christianity. It had a wonderful beginning, a little-known middle, and a glorious end—and millions of people have asked, "What was it all about?" since then.

As God the Father, He authored His story at the beginning of time. As the Son, He brought it to a conclusion and He told us "whodunnit." But, just like those puzzling parables seemed to have more to them, He had more to offer after His death and resurrection. He promised us a sequel. The sequel would be like no other story ever told; it will have a beginning, it might have a middle—but it will never, ever end!

Firstfruits

But every man in his own order: Christ the firstfruits;
afterward they that are Christ's at his coming. . .
1 CORINTHIANS 15:23 KJV

- Name of God the Son

- Jesus is referred to as "firstfruits" twice in the KJV.

- The firstfruits were traditionally the part of a crop, or the part of an increase, which was offered to God as a sacrifice.

- Paul told the church at Corinth that Christ had conquered death and through His victory would come everlasting life for His people.

Throughout the Old Testament, people were directed to offer God their firstfruits—or, the best they had to offer. If they offered wheat, it had to be the freshest, their offerings of bread had to be leavened, and only animals without defect could be sacrificed. It might seem a lot to ask of something that was. . .well, basically going to be destroyed by fire on the altar.

But then God made a sacrifice for us. He didn't say, "I am God, so I don't owe anybody anything"—although He could have, and how could we have argued? He didn't offer us a few years of better harvests or generations of peace, although both were well within His power, and people would have been grateful.

No. Instead of divine gimmicks, He offered the

very best He had to give, His only begotten Son, His own Firstfruits, to be destroyed upon a rough wooden cross. He didn't do it because we begged and pleaded. He didn't do it because He had no other choice. He did it because He loves us and wanted to guarantee our eternal salvation.

Surrounded as we are by that kind of love, how could we possibly offer anything but our very best in return?

Plant of Renown

And I will raise up for them a plant of renown,
and they shall be no more consumed with hunger in the land,
neither bear the shame of the heathen any more.
EZEKIEL 34:29 KJV

- Name of God the Son

- Jesus is referred to as a "plant of renown" once in the KJV.

- The term *Plant of Renown* may have been another way of referring to the Branch of Jesse, a description (and prediction) of the coming Messiah. In talking about being hungry no more, Ezekiel was probably referring to the Plant of Renown satisfying our spiritual hunger.

- Ezekiel reminded the Israelites that, despite present troubles God was still with them and would be their deliverance.

After all the uproar about genetically modified crops, there are still people who think that what the scientists are trying to achieve is a fine and worthwhile goal. The plants they want to "create" will, they hope, thrive in harsher environments, provide a greater yield, and help sustain life. Of course, we wouldn't have to manipulate our agriculture into working overtime if people could be convinced to turn away with war, corruption, and greed, concentrating instead on "Love thy neighbor."

It was a Plant of Renown who gave that advice. The Holy Spirit planted a seed that grew and lived in such a hostile environment that it was killed a mere three years after flowering. But in those three years, it produced a yield of first twelve, then hundreds, and then millions of others. And as for sustaining life, the Plant of Renown sustains lives of renown, and not just until the next harvest—forever!

Wall of Fire

*For I, saith the LORD, will be unto her a wall of fire round about,
and will be the glory in the midst of her.*
ZECHARIAH 2:5 KJV

- Name of God the Father

- God is referred to as a "wall of fire" once in
  the KJV.

- In an age when fireproof materials were all
  but inconceivable, a wall of fire would have
  been considered an unbreachable defense.

- Zechariah was predicting a return to glory for
  Jerusalem—a city once again under God's protection. The scattered Jews would return from
  exile and people of many nations would worship in Jerusalem. It would be a time when God
  would dwell in the city. Zechariah may have
  been predicting Jesus or the Second Coming.

If you have a computer, it is probably protected by a
firewall. When you go online, the firewall filters all
messages, allowing the permissible ones through and
blocking potentially harmful ones.

God, Ezekiel promised, would be that kind of
protection for Jerusalem. It wouldn't need city walls; it
would have a divine Wall of Fire.

The Lord can be a Wall of Fire for our lives, too.
Just activate a program called *prayer*—it's the best firewall around.

Quickening Spirit

And so it is written, The first man Adam was made a living soul;
the last Adam was made a quickening spirit.
1 CORINTHIANS 15:45 KJV

- Name of God the Son

- Jesus is referred to as a "quickening spirit" once in the KJV.

- The term *quicken* means "to come alive" or "to receive life." It also means "to revive," which reminds us that eternal life was the original design for humanity.

- In this verse, Paul differentiated between the natural man, Adam, and the spiritual man, Jesus. Through his creation, Adam *received* life and lived out his days. Jesus came as the *source* of life. He lived out His days—and then continued to live on. And this was the gift He brought for all who believed.

Try as they might, scientists can't shock inert cells into life. And, despite the best efforts and beliefs of "mad scientists," lightning only destroys. God, and only God, is the Quickening Spirit that gives life.

Jesus made it simple. He came to quicken a new kind of life in those who believe, a life that doesn't require lightning or science—only faith. And the life He gives us will never end!

King of Kings

And on His robe and on His thigh He has a name written,
KING OF KINGS AND LORD OF LORDS.
REVELATION 19:16 NASB

- Name of God the Son

- Jesus is referred to as "King of kings" three times in the NASB.

- In empire times, it was not unusual for one ruler to have dominion over many less powerful rulers, but the terms *King of Kings* and *Lord of Lords* are used here to indicate the One to whom *all* rulers should kneel in honor.

- In the book of Revelation, John paints an awesome and terrible vision of Jesus at the Second Coming. His name is The Word of God, but across His blood-soaked robe is the name *King of Kings and Lord of Lords*.

Not a king, but perhaps the most powerful royal ever, Queen Victoria ruled the British Empire at its height, encompassing one-quarter of the world's population. Even so, she knew where true authority lay.

She once wished Jesus would return in her lifetime. When asked why, she replied, "Because I should so love to lay my crown at His blessed feet."

Victoria was wise enough to know who the King of kings—and queens really was.

Jesus of Nazareth

Philip findeth Nathanael, and saith unto him, We have found him,
of whom Moses in the law, and the prophets, did write,
Jesus of Nazareth, the son of Joseph.
JOHN 1:45 KJV

- Name of God the Son

- Jesus is referred to as "Jesus of Nazareth" seventeen times in the KJV.

- Nazareth is the hometown of Jesus. The meaning of the name is disputed, but it may derive from *ne'tser*, meaning "branch," in accordance with the prophecy of Isaiah.

- In this verse, Jesus was gathering His disciples around Him. Nathanael doubted that anything good could come from such a small, unimpressive town, which lends to the reality of how humble Jesus' origins really were.

What's the name of that little town along the road? The place where they're less sophisticated, less cultured, a little. . .unrefined? Imagine you heard that someone from that vicinity claimed to be the savior of mankind. Would you bother going to see them, or would you dismiss them as crazy right then and there?

Nathanael took the second option, but moments after meeting Jesus, he changed his mind! May we be as open-minded when we meet Him.

Power of the Highest

And the angel answered and said unto her, The Holy Ghost shall come upon thee, and the power of the Highest shall overshadow thee: therefore also that holy thing which shall be born of thee shall be called the Son of God.
LUKE 1:35 KJV

- Name of God the Holy Spirit

- The Holy Spirit is referred to as the "power of the Highest" once in the KJV.

- The Holy Spirit is the invisible, but no less powerful, aspect of God the Father.

- In this verse, an angel is telling a surprised young woman that she will bear the child of God.

If God the Father appeared to you, well, you would probably notice Him. Moses certainly did! If Jesus came to visit, you would surely recognize Him. But the Holy Spirit? What would that look like?

When you think of electricity, you might think of power lines, appliances, plugs, and sockets. But these tools simply channel a power that is impossible to see. Nuclear power conjures images of weapons, submarines, and massive power plants; but again, these images merely imply how the energy is distributed—not the energy itself.

Both these energy sources are a part of creation, put in place for our benefit, but they can't be seen.

We only become aware of them through their results. Those results have changed our world. So how much more impressive, how much more world-changing then, would the power of the One who created creation be?

We never see the Holy Spirit, but, like electrical and nuclear powers, the Power of the Highest is visible through its results. And, in the instance the angel was preparing Mary for, those results were wonderful indeed!

Refiner's Fire

But who may abide the day of his coming?
and who shall stand when he appeareth?
for he is like a refiner's fire.
MALACHI 3:2 KJV

- Name of God the Son

- Jesus is referred to as a "refiner's fire" once in the KJV.

- A refiner is someone who heats metal that has been mined from the ground to remove its impurities. Like a refiner's fire, Jesus, too, is a purifying force.

- Malachi was warning the priests in the Temple of Jerusalem that they had better start living what they were teaching because God's Messenger could arrive at any time.

Metals do not come from the earth in a pure state. If you've ever seen iron ore being smelted in a furnace, you probably noticed the violence the process entails. All the action takes place on the surface. It is a turbulent mix of burning black and red slag. But underneath, the iron is getting purer. The slag is the dirt, stone, and other undesirable stuff the iron has been trapped in. Burning the slag and skimming it off is the most effective way to remove it, but it's somewhat reminiscent of hell.

We might rail against the Lord when we suffer,

when we lose, and when our hurt is more than we can bear. But in addition to being a fisher of men, He is a miner of souls. He is trying to extract us from this world. But He doesn't want all our nasty sin to come with us. He wants our purified soul. At the end of the smelting process, iron becomes stronger than it ever was. Likewise, after we are purified, we will be glorious!

Maker

- Name of God the Father

- God is referred to as the "maker" eighteen times in the KJV.

- God, the Maker, made the universe out of nothing and man out of dust.

- Job cursed the day of his birth because of all the "evils" that had befallen him. His friend Eliphaz encouraged him to stay firm in faith to a God who must surely know what He is doing. Of course, God did know what He was doing: He was proving to the devil that an ordinary man of faith would stay firm in his love for the Lord despite Satan's worst works.

There's a joke where scientists challenge God to a creation competition. God takes a handful of dirt and makes a man. Unimpressed, the scientist reaches down. . . . "Ah!" says God. "First, make your own dirt!"

Mankind makes lots of impressive stuff. But he is simply rearranging the raw materials the Maker provided. So where does God's work stop and man's stuff begin? It never happens. Even man is part of the work of the Maker.

Shade

The LORD is thy keeper: the LORD is thy shade upon thy right hand.
PSALM 121:5 KJV

- Name of God the Father

- God is referred to as "shade" once in the KJV.

- The term *right-hand man* usually means your most dependable friend or your most able helper. In this instance, God will be close enough to cast a shadow on your right hand, and He is both your Friend and your Helper.

- In one of the most comforting passages of the Bible, the psalm writer (probably King David) assured us that God does not sleep and protects us by day and by night. He will preserve us at our going out and our coming in, and He will protect us "for evermore" (Psalm 121:8 KJV).

Shade from the sun is more important, and more subtle, than most people realize. Without the earth's magnetic field being in place, powerful solar winds would have long ago stripped the atmosphere from our planet. And why does the Earth have a magnetic field when it isn't a magnet? Albert Einstein described this as one of the greatest mysteries in physics.

It's either a great mystery, or the Lord is indeed a very great Shade.

Shield

*For thou, L*ORD*, wilt bless the righteous;*
with favour wilt thou compass him as with a shield.
PSALM 5:12 KJV

- Name of God the Father

- God is referred to as being or providing a "shield" twenty-one times in the KJV.

- A shield is a tool of protection, typically in battle.

- King David must have been having a hard time with double-dealers. In Psalm 5, he prays that God will allow deceitful, evil people to fall by their own misdeeds and that God will protect those who are walking the straight and narrow path as if with a shield.

The verse is also a statement of King David's devotion, and a call for those who share it to rejoice in the protection of the Lord.

Baylor University once carried out a survey on attitudes toward religion. In this seemingly increasingly secular world, more than half the adults surveyed felt they had been protected by angels at some time in their lives. Even more amazingly, 20 percent of those who claimed no religion felt they had been similarly protected.

Despite the world's denials, God is still at work. In many ways, He remains a Shield for the righteous.

Gift of God

Jesus answered and said unto her, If thou knewest the gift of God, and who it is that saith to thee, Give me to drink; thou wouldest have asked of him, and he would have given thee living water.

JOHN 4:10 KJV

- Name of God the Son

- Jesus is referred to as the "gift of God" twice in the KJV.

- Jesus is the epitome of all that God had to offer mankind, and the foundation of a new covenant. A true gift indeed!

- Jesus was speaking to the woman by the well. His disciples had left just before she arrived (as if it had been planned!). He told her the Messiah stood in front of her. Completely convinced, she became an unacknowledged apostle to the Samaritans.

Do you write a thank-you note when you receive a gift?

There's no denying that God truly blesses us with many gifts: babies, spouses, love, singing, stars, gainful employment, memories, community, etc., etc.

Actually we tend to give God less appreciation than He deserves because almost *everything* is a gift from God. You couldn't write enough thank-you notes for all that. . .so why not send Him a thank-you *life*?

Morning Star

I am the root and the offspring of David,
and the bright and morning star.
REVELATION 22:16 KJV

- Name of God the Son

- Jesus refers to himself as the "morning star" twice in Revelation.

- The morning star is traditionally recognized as the bright, distinctive "star" (actually the planet Venus) that appears just before sunrise.

- In the book of Revelation, Jesus affirmed His lineage from King David. He also said that those who obey His commandments will be rewarded with eternal life while those who didn't would be left outside. Almost as a seal upon this promise, and perhaps signifying the dawning of a new way, He calls Himself "the bright and morning star."

Traditionally Venus is referred to as the morning star. The planet often appears in the eastern sky as the brightest "star," most visible as night fades and morning approaches. For peoples across the ages, Venus signaled that night was over and the new day had come.

Jesus fulfills the same role for us. His life signified the end of dark times when sin reigned supreme, and the beginning of new life in the light of God's forgiveness.

Horn of Salvation

Blessed be the Lord God of Israel; for he hath visited and redeemed his people, and hath raised up an horn of salvation for us in the house of his servant David.
LUKE 1:68–69 KJV

- Name of God the Son

- Jesus is referred to as the "horn of salvation" once in the KJV.

- The horn was a symbol of strength and also of anointing.

- After the birth of his son, John, Zechariah uses his newly restored voice to praise God and predict the coming of Jesus.

The horn plays various roles in the Bible. In Exodus, a blast from a horn let people know they might approach the mountain where God dwelt. Samuel anointed Saul with oil from a horn. Zadok the priest performed the same ceremony for Solomon.

When the Tabernacle was being raised in the time of Moses, an altar was built of bronze-overlaid acacia wood. At each corner was a horn where the priests would offer blood sacrifices. A tradition arose that people might seek sanctuary in the Tabernacle and be protected while they clung to a horn. In a real way, these horns were the people's salvation. But, as with all things man-made, the tradition wasn't perfect. Solomon had Joab killed while he clung to one of the horns, hoping to be spared.

Jesus is the way to approach the Father, so He wonderfully fulfills the role of the announcing horn. He is God's anointed like no other ever was, and those who cling to Him—even though the world be against them—will find salvation that no other power can ever take away.

Husband

Behold, the days come, saith the LORD, that I will make a new covenant with the house of Israel, and with the house of Judah: Not according to the covenant that I made with their fathers in the day that I took them by the hand to bring them out of the land of Egypt; which my covenant they brake, although I was an husband unto them, saith the LORD.
JEREMIAH 31:31–32 KJV

- Name of God the Father

- God is referred to as a "husband" twice in the KJV.

- *Husband* is an old Norse term for a house-holder.

- In this verse, God made a new covenant, writing His commandments in the people's hearts.

Referring to God as a Husband and His Church as the Bride is a problem for some men. But, as is usually the case with God, His expectations aren't the same as ours. Guys needn't worry about wearing a dress to the wedding! The sole expectation of the Bride is love and adoration for the Husband.

The old term for a husband, *husbonda*, meant "house-holder" in days when a home was built and defended with physical strength. While some men might still protect their own homes that way, the wise ones rely on faith for their family's security.

When it comes to securing the whole world by

his strength, what man would be arrogant or foolish enough to take that on? Relax, guys. When it comes to the marriage between heaven and earth, settle for the loving role—because when it comes to being the Husband, God really is the only man for the job!

Father of Lights

*Every good gift and every perfect gift is from above,
and cometh down from the Father of lights,
with whom is no variableness, neither shadow of turning.*
JAMES 1:17 KJV

- Name of God the Father

- The name *Father of Lights* refers to God as
  the Creator of the original light, and the
  source from which the light of all good things
  shines.

- Surprisingly, James tells the followers of
  Jesus to rejoice when they are tempted or
  when bad things happen to them. They must
  be on the right path if Satan feels the need
  to attack them. And they can be sure these
  things come from Satan, because nothing but
  good flows from the Father of Lights. In that
  certainty they can rest assured.

The oldest-known hymn is "Phos Hilaron," which
refers to God as the Gladdening Light. Third-
century monks sang it as they lit their evening candles.

God was Father to physical light at the beginning
of time, but, more importantly, He was Father to the
spiritual light of Jesus. Each time we show someone
His love, we light a candle as surely as the monks did.

And God is Father to all those little, wonderful,
lights!

Manna

And the house of Israel called the name thereof Manna.
Exodus 16:31 KJV

- Name of God the Father

- The original meaning of *manna* is not known, although it may simply be a version of the Egyptian term *mennu*, meaning food.

- Having left slavery—and regular meals—behind in Egypt, the Israelites were starving in the desert. So God sent them a special "bread." It appeared with the dew every morning and seemed to evaporate in the sun. Unless it was specially prepared for the Sabbath, it never lasted longer than a day, but there was always enough to feed the hungry people of God. Of course, those same people soon began to take it for granted.

*M*anna. A miraculous food!

But is Manna any more amazing than one seed eventually being able to cover miles of farmland with fresh new corn? Or more amazing than a two-thousand-year-old seed from Herod's temple successfully germinating in 2005?

We are surrounded by food miracles so commonplace that we take them for granted.

God is not only food for our soul, but in many wonderful ways, He is also food for our stomachs as well!

Advocate

My little children, these things I write to you,
so that you may not sin. And if anyone sins,
we have an Advocate with the Father,
Jesus Christ the righteous.
1 JOHN 2:1 NKJV

- Name of God the Son

- Jesus is referred to as "Advocate" once in the NKJV.

- An advocate is one who speaks in support of another, often in a court of law.

- John reminds his readers and listeners that claiming to believe in Christ means following His example. They likely won't achieve that high standard, but if they fail at trying, Jesus will speak up for them at the final judgment.

Perhaps Hollywood's favorite advocate was Atticus Finch. Played by Gregory Peck in *To Kill a Mockingbird*, Atticus defends a man in a hopeless situation because he knows it is the right thing to do. In one scene he tells his children, "You never really understand a person until you consider things from his point of view—until you climb into his skin and walk around in it."

When we finally answer for our lives before God, there is a very good chance we'll be disappointed in ourselves. The pressures of life and the failings of human nature ensure that we'll fall short of Jesus' model of an ideal life. How could a heavenly judge, who has never known the same pressures, possibly understand?

Well, He will. Because through His Son, Jesus Christ, God came down from heaven and walked around as a human for more than thirty years. Atticus thought it was a good idea in theory, but Jesus lived and died the concept just so He could be our Advocate!

Jesus

And she shall bring forth a son, and thou shalt call his name JESUS: for he shall save his people from their sins.
MATTHEW 1:21 KJV

- Name of God the Son

- The name "Jesus" appears 973 times in the KJV.

- *Jesus* is the Greek translation of a name that may have been pronounced *Yeshua*.

- In this verse, the angel explained to Joseph the importance of the son Mary would soon bear him.

It is only fitting that the Lord of all the world would be known by many names—but what did His friends call Him? Actually we can't be sure, but there are plenty of theories.

The name we read as Jesus comes from an Old English translation of a Greek translation of a Hebrew name. To further complicate things, it has been suggested that the English alphabet at the time of translation had no letter *J*. Neither did the Hebrew alphabet. And the Greek alphabet didn't have a *sh* sound, so it substituted *S*.

As far back as Isaiah, it was predicted the Messiah's name would be Immanuel. So why did everyone call Him Jesus instead? Well, they probably didn't.

By reversing the translations, we arrive at a name

similar to Joshua, or Yeshua (remember, no letter *J*.) It's possible that Yeshua is a shortened version of *yeOshUa*, which means "help of Jehovah." Immanuel means "God with us." And why was He with us? To save us. Wouldn't that be the "help of Jehovah"?

In the end, it doesn't matter what His friends called Him or how the name has been translated. What matters is that we love Him and call Him Savior!

The Christ

Thou art the Christ, the Son of the living God.
MATTHEW 16:16 KJV

- Name of God the Son

- Jesus is referred to as "the Christ" nineteen times in the KJV.

- *Christ*, or *Christos*, is the Greek version of "Messiah," or "Anointed One."

- This was a profound statement of faith by Peter at a time when people thought Jesus might be many other things.

Some things never change!

"Whom do men say that I the Son of man am?" (Matthew 16:13 KJV). Jesus asked His disciples. John the Baptist was a popular choice. Or Elijah. Or Jeremiah. Or some other prophet. People were confused. And they still are!

Ask people the same question today, and you will get different (but no less varied) answers. Some settle for Him simply being a good, wise man; some have Him being a transcendent guru of sorts—an Essene, a crazy man, a figment of cultural imagination. . . .

Peter walked away from his livelihood for this man. So did the other eleven followers. They ate, slept, and lived with Him. If any group were well positioned to determine what or who He was, it would have been these fellows. After His execution, they ran away—

but they came back! Each of them stayed the course, facing ridicule, persecution, and (all except John) violent deaths. They knew the man and knew He was worth dedicating their lives to. Why else would they have done all they did?

Now, as then, people quibble over who Jesus was, but for those who really know Him, Peter's answer is the only one that suffices. He is "the Christ, the Son of the living God."

Buckler

As for God, his way is perfect: the word of the LORD is tried:
he is a buckler to all those that trust in him.
PSALM 18:30 KJV

- Name of God the Father

- Bucklers are referred to frequently in the Old Testament, but the Lord is called "a buckler" five times.

- A buckler is a small shield, usually made of leather with brass or iron decorations.

- King David was singing his praises to the Lord when he referred to Him as "a buckler" in Psalm 18.

A buckler has nothing to do with buckles. It's actually just a small round shield.

What does it mean then when the Bible talks about going into battle with your buckler *and* your shield? The people of Israel had to fight for everything they had (except the love of God). It was a hard and often bloody existence. So it's no surprise they were usually proficient with a variety of weaponry and defenses. A larger shield was just the thing to hide behind when arrows or spears rained down, but they were a bit clumsy when it came to hand-to-hand combat.

The buckler though, at around two feet in diameter, could deflect a sword stroke and be used to strike a powerful blow to the enemy in return.

What does this have to do with God? Well, it shows He is not just a god of ceremonies and temples. As King David knew, when the going gets really tough— when it's a matter of life and death and there is no one else between you and your enemy—God will be at hand, protecting and striking as required to preserve a faithful servant. He will be your Buckler.

Savior

"The LORD lives! Praise be to my Rock!
Exalted be my God, the Rock, my Savior!"
2 SAMUEL 22:47 NIV

- Name of God the Son

- God, or the living God, is referred to as "Savior" many times in the Bible, and Jesus is predicted in the Old Testament by the same name. But there are at least fifteen instances in the New Testament where the term *Savior* is specifically directed at the person of Jesus.

- The word *Savior* means "the One who saves us."

- In his song, David thanks God for delivering him from his enemies.

Read through the Old Testament, and you will find many references to God as the Savior. He was the One the Israelites called on in their times of need (and then usually forgot about afterward). He was Israel's Savior. But what about the rest of the world?

Well, (as far as anyone can read the mind of God) it seems the Israelites were to represent Him to the world—proclaim Him, if you like. But time and again, they neglected this holy calling.

The time came when God had to actually come down and visit this "stiff-necked" people and show them the full extent of His love. But how could such powerful love reside with just one people? The Samaritan woman at the well became known as Photini ("the enlightener") because she carried Jesus' message of salvation to people other than the Jews. Saul became Paul and carried the message throughout the known world.

What was the message? That the Savior had arrived. He is here now, and not only for a lucky few. Jesus Christ came to be the Savior of the whole world.

Righteous Servant

He shall see of the travail of his soul, and shall be satisfied:
by his knowledge shall my righteous servant justify many;
for he shall bear their iniquities.
Isaiah 53:11 KJV

- Name of God the Son

- Jesus is referred to as "righteous servant" once in the KJV.

- A righteous servant is a good and faithful servant.

- In these verses, Isaiah predicts the life, death, and resurrection of Jesus.

He shall see of the travail of his soul." What does that mean?

Travail generally means "hardship" these days, but it used to mean "torture" or "torment." Do you think the Lord was ever tortured in heaven? It's hard to imagine. But He gave all of that up and became completely human in a body destined for a death designed by the Romans for its shock value.

Was He scared? So scared He sweated blood over it! Did He have to do it? He's the Lord of the universe— He didn't have to do anything! He did it all as the ultimate sacrifice to God and so that through "the travail of his soul," He might understand our weaknesses and be better able to speak for us on Judgment Day. He did it for our salvation.

As His fate on earth loomed over Him, Jesus expressed His fear, but He also understood that it doesn't matter what He wanted. In dying on the cross for our salvation, He became our Righteous Servant. And we ought to ask ourselves—can we be any less for Him?

Lord of the Harvest

Pray ye therefore the Lord of the harvest,
that he will send forth labourers into his harvest.
MATTHEW 9:38 KJV

- Name of God the Son

- Jesus is referred to as the "Lord of the harvest" twice in the KJV.

- The Lord of the Harvest plants the seeds of faith in human hearts.

- Luke was recounting how Jesus sent seventy disciples out to the cities He planned to visit.

Scattering seed on the ground isn't the same as making them grow. You tend the soil and water it, but you don't make it grow. There's something in the seed, placed in the very first seed by the Creator, that actually makes the thing grow. But your efforts certainly help.

In the same way, you might talk to a hundred people about faith, and only one will end up coming to church with you. You might think that's a pretty poor return for your efforts, but you never know when, or in what other heart, the memory of your words will sprout into a green shoot. That's God doing His bit. But if you don't sow the seed in the first place, it won't grow!

"The harvest truly is plenteous, but the labourers are few" (Matthew 9:37 KJV). In other words, the harvest is eternal life for all. But for there to be a harvest, the seeds need to be sown. Why not cast a few? You can plant ideas at home, at work, amongst strangers you meet—and then get on with the rest of your life. The Lord of the Harvest will take it from there!

Covenant of the People

*I the LORD have called thee in righteousness, and will hold thine hand,
and will keep thee, and give thee for a covenant of the people,
for a light of the Gentiles.*
ISAIAH 42:6 KJV

- Name of God the Son

- Jesus is referred to as the "covenant of the people" twice in the KJV.

- The Covenant of the People was a living example of the relationship between God and humanity.

- Isaiah was prophesying the coming of a Servant of the Lord who would save the Israelites but would also save the Gentiles— which was a radical departure for Hebrew prophets.

Across the world, empires and countries would demonstrate faith in their neighbors and extend trust through the exchange of hostages and prisoners. Sometimes it was civilized; the hostages would be sons and daughters of royalty, and they would be given allowances and an honored role in society. This was the human covenant nations made with each other. But if either side betrayed their part of the bargain, the consequences could be fatal.

Jesus was the human face of God's covenant with humanity. He came here knowing that we would not keep our side of the bargain; after all, we had been letting God down for generations. Still, He came. He came willingly, and He died because of our treachery—to show us how much the covenant meant to God.

Forerunner

*Whither the forerunner is for us entered, even Jesus, made an high
priest for ever after the order of Melchisedec.*
HEBREWS 6:20 KJV

- Name of God the Son

- Jesus is referred to as the "forerunner" once
  in the KJV.

- The forerunner is one who goes on ahead,
  usually blazing a trail and making it safe for
  others to follow.

- The author of Hebrews prays his listeners will
  not hold firm to old rituals, but move forward
  in the perfect way shown by Christ. Those
  who hear the message and do not reform
  their practices, he says, will put Christ to
  shame. But God has promised better things
  for the faithful followers of Jesus. And, as he
  points out, God cannot lie!

Who is our forerunner and where has he gone?
Jesus was the Forerunner, and He went beyond the veil of death. What happened there no one
really knows, but we do know Jesus overcame death,
and just as He rose again, so shall we.

Beyond death's former empire is the Father's
house. The Forerunner got there first, and He has prepared a home for us. All we slower runners have to do
is get there!

Father of Mercies

Blessed be God, even the Father of our Lord Jesus Christ,
the Father of mercies, and the God of all comfort.
2 CORINTHIANS 1:3 KJV

- Name of God the Father

- God is referred to as the "Father of mercies" once in the KJV.

- The name the *Father of Mercies* translates into Hebrew as *Avi HaRachamim.*

- Paul began his second letter to the Corinthians in the same way he began the first—by praising God.

In a politically correct age, some people have called the idea of God the Father a misogynistic construct. Why, they want to know, couldn't He be God the Mother? Actually, both names limit the Creator. He is beyond stereotypes. The labels we attach to Him are more for our benefit than His.

The name Father of Mercies is a perfect example of how God can satisfy both sides of the gender argument. It begins with the Hebrew word *avi,* which is masculine. It means "father." But then we have *rachamim* (or *rahamin*), which has been translated as "mercy" *and* as "compassion." But it means a specific type of compassion: the type of compassion a mother feels for the child of her womb. Is there a stronger bond in the whole world? That's how God loves us.

This combination of the masculine and the feminine encompasses the paternal urge to protect us and push us to be better than we think we can be; and the maternal urge to love us, to forgive us endlessly, and even to die for us!

God the Father? God the Mother? The Father of Mercies is more than either—and loves like both!

Fullers' Soap

*But who may abide the day of his coming? and who shall stand
when he appeareth? for he is like. . .fullers' soap.*
MALACHI 3:2 KJV

- Name of God the Son

- Jesus is referred to as "fullers' soap" once in
  the KJV.

- Fullers cleaned and thickened woolen
  materials, thus making them "fuller."
  Their soap was an alkali made from plant
  ashes. The Fullers' Field, where this work
  traditionally took place, lies to the west of
  Jerusalem.

- Malachi records God's promise that the
  arrival of "the LORD, whom ye seek. . .the
  messenger of the covenant," (Malachi 3:1 KJV)
  was imminent, and when He arrived, no man
  would be able to stand against Him.

Woven material was given to the fuller in its raw
state. He would boil it, rinse, add soap, and
stamp on it. Repeatedly. The end result was a clean,
tight, wind-resistant material.

So the cloth gets into hot water and trampled on
but ends up a new, improved version of itself. Doesn't
that sound like a life of faith? With Jesus washing us
like Fullers' Soap we can only shine brighter at the end.

Portion

The portion of Jacob is not like them: for he is the former
of all things; and Israel is the rod of his inheritance:
The LORD of hosts is his name.
JEREMIAH 10:16 KJV

- Name of God the Son.

- Jesus is referred to as the "portion" of Jacob
  once in the KJV.

- A *portion* can either mean "an inheritance" or
  "something allotted to an individual by God."

- Jeremiah was railing against the idol worship
  of both his own people and the Babylonians.
  He assured them all that the real thing was
  on His way.

Jeremiah wasn't a subtle man. He spent a quarter of
a century warning Judah about its downfall. In that
time, he walked the streets with a yoke around his neck,
got imprisoned, and was thrown in a pit to die. He
prayed so often for his people that he even tried God's
patience. Amazingly, God told Jeremiah to, "Pray no
more for these people, Jeremiah. Do not weep or pray
for them, for I will not listen to them when they cry out
to me in distress."

Sounds harsh, doesn't it? After all, aren't you sup-
posed to turn to God in your hour of need? Maybe
God only wanted a rest from Jeremiah's prayers because He knew the peoples of Judah and Israel must

suffer awhile. And because He knew help was already on the way. Help was "the former of all things" and had been on His way since before Creation.

We can only suppose God shared the information with Jeremiah. How else would the worried prophet have known that the Portion of Jacob would make it all right in the end?

Refuge

For thou hast been. . .a refuge from the storm. . .
when the blast of the terrible ones is as a storm against the wall.
ISAIAH 25:4 KJV

- Name of God the Father

- God is referred to as a "refuge" 61 times in the KJV.

- A refuge is a place that offers shelter from danger.

- Isaiah is proclaiming the power and might of God. He tempers this by rejoicing in the shelter God offers to the faithful. He goes on to say how God will overcome death.

A young English curate was out walking when he was caught in a sudden thunderstorm. Rushing to a nearby rocky crag, he found shelter in a cave. Marveling slightly at this shelter being available to him just when he needed it, he searched his pockets for a scrap of paper. He had none, but the wind blew a playing card at his feet. He picked it up and wrote, "Rock of ages, cleft for me."

His hasty scribble went on to become one of the world's most famous hymns. That should be no surprise, because just like Augustus Toplady, the young curate, generation after generation of Christians have found God to be their shelter in their time of greatest need.

Who is to say that rock face wasn't "cleft" for Reverend Toplady, just so he would have a refuge from that particular storm? That's the good thing about a God who is also Lord of Time and Space. He knows what you are going to need and when you will need it, and He is more than capable of preparing your refuge years in advance!

Desire of All Nations

And I will shake all nations, and the desire of all nations shall come: and I will fill this house with glory, saith the LORD of hosts.
HAGGAI 2:7 KJV

- Name of God the Son

- Jesus is referred to as the "desire of all nations" once in the KJV.

- Charles Spurgeon suggests that the word *desire* may, in this instance, more accurately be interpreted as "the elect" or "the desirable ones."

- The prophet Haggai was instructed by God to tell the governor of Judah, its priests, and the remnants of its people, that even though the country and the people were devastated, He had not rejected them, and greater times lay ahead.

Haggai may well have been talking here about the times that would follow the Second Coming. Then, according to Spurgeon's interpretation, the whole world would be shaken and the faithful would leave behind earthly allegiances, coming together as God's eternal Church.

So you might ask how the Desire of All Nations became a name of Jesus. The answer is simply this: the faithful, the desirable ones, only become so through having Jesus in their hearts!

God Who Sees

And she called the name of the LORD that spake unto her,
Thou God seest me: for she said, Have I also here
looked after him that seeth me?
GENESIS 16:13 KJV

- Name of God the Father

- There are many references to people being in the sight of God in the KJV.

- The name *God Who Sees* reminds us that we are always under the watchful care of our heavenly Father.

- Hagar, having conceived Abram's child, ran away from his wife, Sarai. On her way, she encountered an angel—or God Himself in the form of an angel. They met by a spring, which she named *Beer Lahai Roi*, or "the well of the Living One who sees me."

Gods of mythology used devices, like pools of water or mirrors, to watch mankind. God just sees. And He doesn't just see some things—because He is in everything, He sees everything!

Encountering a scared Hagar on the run, God asked her where she had come from and where she was going. Surely He was just making conversation. If He didn't already know the answers to those questions, He would not have been exactly where He needed to be at exactly the time He needed to be there.

Not only did He see the newly conceived son in her womb, but he saw the generations that would come from him. Then He told Hagar her son would be called Ishmael, which means "God hears."

Despite seeing everything we do—good and bad— God still loves us. That ought to be all the encouragement we need to live better lives.

Spirit of Glory

*If ye be reproached for the name of Christ, happy are ye;
for the spirit of glory and of God resteth upon you:
on their part he is evil spoken of, but on your part he is glorified.*
1 PETER 4:14 KJV

- Name of God the Holy Spirit

- The Holy Spirit is referred to as the "spirit of glory" once in the KJV.

- The Spirit of Glory is the essence of self-sacrifice.

- Peter reminded his readers and listeners that the life of a Christ-follower was meant to be one of testing rather than comfort.

In any conflict between good and evil, those on the negative side will have a range of reasons for being there—power, hurt, greed, feelings of entitlement, lust, having been deceived, self-loathing, fear, and so on. Those on the positive side will generally have one reason—love!

But who ever heard of anyone actively supporting fear, lust, or greed with their life? All of the disciples met gruesome deaths (except Judas, who hanged himself and John, who died of old age). They could have walked away at any time. What gave them the strength to keep going in the face of torture and execution? The Spirit of Glory did.

Countless people have followed in their footsteps

132

since then. How many have been willing martyrs for the enemy's side? Love wins because, divorced from self, it doesn't stop when the body does. The Spirit of Glory makes that kind of sacrifice (and all the littler sacrifices along the way) possible by reminding us that nothing but glory awaits us on the other side of the veil known as death.

Daysman

Neither is there any daysman betwixt us,
that might lay his hand upon us both.
JOB 9:33 KJV

- Name of God the Son

- The term "daysman" is used once in the KJV.

- Job probably wasn't referring to Jesus when he used the word *daysman*, but that is what He became.

Before the judicial system was established in England, appealing to the court was an expensive and time-consuming business. It was generally a privilege only the gentry and upper class could afford.

So the daysman system was established. The daysman was someone local who served as a mediator for every kind of dispute and brought both parties in disagreement to a binding conclusion within twenty-four hours.

Job wished desperately for someone to put his case to God. But who was there who could possibly be lowly enough to understand his complaint and high enough to address it to the Almighty? No one.

Then came Jesus!

When we reach the ultimate court, the Court of Final Judgment, we will have One who lived both as man and as God to arbitrate on our behalf. Our very own Daysman will see we receive a fair and merciful judgment on that glorious day.

Captain of Their Salvation

For it became him, for whom are all things, and by whom are all things, in bringing many sons unto glory, to make the captain of their salvation perfect through sufferings.
HEBREWS 2:10 KJV

- Name of God the Son

- Jesus is referred to as the "captain of their salvation" once in the KJV.

- A captain is a person who is at the head of or who has authority over others.

- The writer of Hebrews explained how it was God's will that Jesus suffer on earth and taste death for the sake of every man. The experience joined Jesus with all of mankind, and those who followed Him should not be ashamed to declare His name amongst themselves or to the world.

Alexander the Great believed a good captain never asked his men to do anything he himself wouldn't do. In that same spirit Jesus showed us how to live in a world hostile to His message. Then He died to show us that the path to salvation lay beyond death.

Like any great captain, Jesus never asks us to do anything He hasn't already done, and like the bravest of them, He went "over the top" first.

The Door

I am the door: by me if any man enter in, he shall be saved, and shall go in and out, and find pasture.
JOHN 10:9 KJV

- Name of God the Son

- Jesus refers to himself as "the door" twice and as "standing by the door" twice in the KJV.

- "I am the door" tells us that the only way to God is through Jesus Christ.

- Jesus tells the parable of the Good Shepherd in John 10 when He refers to Himself as The Door.

There is a famous painting by the Pre-Raphaelite artist William Holman Hunt called "The Light of the World." A robed Jesus Christ stands outside a door with a lamp in one hand. He wears two crowns: the crown of glory and the crown of thorns. His free hand is raised as if he is about to knock on the door. The hinges are rusted, and the bottom half of the door is overgrown with wildflowers and brambles, suggesting there hasn't been much traffic through it.

A detail that isn't often noticed by the casual observer, but which was surely a deliberate omission on the part of Hunt, is that there is no handle on the outside of the door. Jesus can't simply open it and walk in. The door can only be opened from the inside by the occupant of the house. Jesus will knock—but He has to be invited in!

"Light of the World" is a metaphor, but the point is an important one. In real life, Jesus is how we get to God. He actually is The Door—but *we* are the ones who have to step through!

Living God

And the king spake and said. . .O Daniel,
servant of the living God, is thy God, whom thou servest
continually, able to deliver thee from the lions?
DANIEL 6:20 KJV

- Name of God the Father

- God is referred to as the "living God" thirty times in the KJV.

- "Living God" in Hebrew is *Elohim Chayim*.

- Daniel, one of the exiles from Judah, had done well in the court of King Darius. So well that others plotted against him. Deceived by his advisers and against his better judgement, King Darius ordered Daniel to be thrown into a den of lions for worshipping the Living God. Daniel's faith was so strong that angels closed the mouths of the hungry lions, and he was completely unharmed.

So the Israelites worshipped a calf made of gold. Nothing new there! Tribes across the world have worshipped a variety of inanimate objects. The Greek and the Roman gods had more personality, but they tended to be distant, living far away on Mount Olympus.

The Living God is different. He lived amongst His people and traveled the desert with them. Then He wrote His commandments in their hearts—and came to reside there!

Jehovahshalom

And the LORD said unto him, Peace be unto thee; fear not:
thou shalt not die. Then Gideon built an altar there unto the LORD,
and called it Jehovahshalom.
JUDGES 6:23–24 KJV

- Name of God the Father

- "Jehovahshalom" is referred to once in the
  KJV.

- *Jehovahshalom* means the "Lord is Peace" or
  "the Lord our Peace."

- An angel of the Lord visited Gideon, telling
  him he would be a leader of his people.
  When Gideon prepared an offering, the angel
  touched it with a staff, and it went up in
  flames.

Peace! It seems like something everyone would want. But it has been suggested that in 3,500 years, there have been only 286 years without a war being fought somewhere. Maybe it's not such a simple thing after all. Sustained peace seems almost to be beyond man's capabilities.

Perhaps it is. A generation after the Fall, Cain committed murder. That would have been unthinkable in Eden, but war and destruction have been with us ever since. What made the difference? Well, in Eden we walked with God.

Gideon knew God would keep His promise of

peace. Gideon knew He *was* peace. That's why he gave his altar the name he did.

If we want to start raising that tally of peaceful years until they equal and then surpass the recorded years of war, mankind has to get beside God again. But until mankind gets its act together, each of us, like Gideon, can accept the Lord's personal gift of peace in our hearts as we move through this world of troubles— until we finally arrive in heaven, where He will be forever Jehovahshalom, the Lord our Peace.

Last Adam

So it is written: "The first man Adam became a living being";
the last Adam, a life-giving spirit.
1 CORINTHIANS 15:45 NIV

- Name of God the Son

- Jesus is referred to as the "last Adam" once in the NIV.

- All generations, ever since Eden, have come from a man and a woman. Adam was the first to come directly from God. Jesus was the last.

- Paul addressed the question of resurrection with the Corinthians, using the example of a seed which dies to its previous nature before bringing forth a new plant. Our earthly, physical bodies he compares to the seed, suggesting that though our physical bodies die, that is a necessary step in giving birth to our perfect spiritual bodies.

Adam was a perfect man. Unfortunately that perfection included the free will to give into temptation. He was tempted—and couldn't resist. The bond between God and His creation was broken.

God has been trying ever since to reestablish that bond. But we kept messing up.

So God sent another perfect man. He could be tempted, too. And He was, terribly! But Jesus resisted. He maintained the link with God and reestablished it for Adam's children.

The Word

In the beginning was the Word, and the Word was with God,
and the Word was God.
JOHN 1:1 KJV

- Name of God the Son

- "The Word" is only capitalized and used as a name six times, all of them in John or 1 John.

- *The Word* is a translation of the Greek word *logos*, which means "word," "discourse," or "reason."

- Perhaps for the first time in the Gospel, John stresses the full implications of Jesus' divinity in the first verse of his book. At around the same time, Philo of Alexandria was using the same term to describe the aspect of God that "is the bond of everything, holding all things together."

If *logos* means "discourse," then we have to think that Jesus was God's way of communicating with us—His way of explaining Himself and His connection to us. The life of Christ was certainly a persuasive and powerful argument!

But surely The Word of God is all around us: in everything we see and everything we are. The whole of creation is His message to us, and John tells us that The Word was with God from the beginning. The beginning was when God started creating. And if we believe Philo of Alexandria, The Word is the stuff the universe is created from.

Perhaps it's all part of God's message to us, but the whole of creation is just too big, too loud, for us to decipher. Wonderful and amazing as creation is, perhaps the life of Christ was simply God reiterating that He did all this for us—only this time He whispered so we could hear.

Spirit That Was upon Moses

And the Lord came down in a cloud, and spake unto him,
and took of the spirit that was upon him [Moses],
and gave it unto the seventy elders: and it came to pass,
that, when the spirit rested upon them,
they prophesied, and did not cease.
NUMBERS 11:25 KJV

- Name of God the Holy Spirit

- "The spirit that was upon him [Moses]"
  appears once in the KJV.

- The Spirit That Was upon Moses was the
  strength of the Lord working through him.

- Moses had asked for help, and the Lord
  created seventy helpers for him.

Why do I have to do everything for people who
won't help themselves and don't appreciate
me?" was more or less Moses' complaint to God.
Sound familiar?

There are people in this world who help others,
and then there are those who choose to focus on themselves. What's the difference? Well, the first group have
God in their hearts. Whether they realize it or not,
God *is* the strength that bears not only their load but
the burdens of others as well.

Moses may have thought he was pulling his own
load, but when he despaired, God showed him the

source of his strength. He gave seventy others the same "spirit" that had been keeping Moses going.

We are at our weakest when we think we have only ourselves to rely on and that we are the only ones who can do it. When you feel like giving up—don't. Ask God to send help, and give others a chance to share the Spirit That Was upon Moses (and you!)

Lord Who Heals

*And [God] said, If thou wilt diligently hearken to the voice of
the LORD thy God. . .I will put none of these diseases upon thee,
which I have brought upon the Egyptians:
for I am the LORD that healeth thee.*
EXODUS 15:26 KJV

- Name of God the Father

- God is referred to as the Lord who Heals, or
  the "Lord that healeth," once in the KJV.

- By referring to Himself as the "Lord that
  healeth," God was juxtaposing what He
  planned to do *for* the Israelites and what He
  had done *to* the Egyptians.

- God had just told Moses how to purify the
  bitter waters of Marah, and then He promised
  He would be the One who healed the
  Israelites—if they stayed faithful!

G reat truths are found in simple examples.
Imagine you fall and cut your hand. The cut
will bleed, washing out foreign bodies and reducing the
chances of infection. The blood takes oxygen and nu-
trients to the wound, because they will be needed for
the healing process. Bruises and swelling are nothing
more than signs that the wound is beginning to repair
itself! Damaged tissue dies. As it dies, it forms a bar-
rier behind which new tissue can safely grow. Then the
wound closes. It closes from the inside out, which is

another deterrent to infection. It's a perfect and complex process. Who organized all that?

Scientists are on the verge of making machines that can repair themselves—maybe—but it takes a lot of intelligence, research, effort, and money to even begin to make that happen. Atheists will suggest the "machine" that is your body came about by random accident. But we know who's really responsible. Thank the Lord today for healing our ills and our imperfect hearts from the inside out!

Potentate

Which in his times he shall shew, who is the blessed and only
Potentate, the King of kings, and Lord of lords.
1 TIMOTHY 6:15 KJV

- Name of God the Son

- Jesus is referred to as "Potentate" once in the KJV.

- A potentate is one having authority over others—a term most often applied to Middle Eastern rulers.

- Timothy was urging his readers to be content with their situation in life, realizing and accepting that faith and a good witness are far more important things than wealth and position. When the Potentate, before whom all other powers are nothing, returns, He won't look at whether we were "successful" or not but at whether we fought the good fight or not.

It's easy to see Jesus as Potentate. In Latin *potent* means "powerful" or "authoritative." Another interpretation uses the Middle English word *potente*. And in *The Canterbury Tales*, Chaucer wrote that the Summoner *leyde adoun His potente*: he laid aside his crutch!

Quite a different meaning, but how appropriate! Christ never uses His power to oppress. He uses it to support. He is an authority *and* a crutch. A Potentate in every sense of the word!

Judge of All the Earth

That be far from thee to do after this manner, to slay the righteous with the wicked. . . . Shall not the Judge of all the earth do right?
GENESIS 18:25 KJV

- Name of God the Father

- God is referred to as "Judge of all the earth" once in the KJV.

- In the Hebrew tradition, a judge was a leader of the people who was required to seek justice above all else.

- God visited Abraham to tell him he would have a son in his old age. Immediately afterward, God planned to destroy Sodom and Gomorrah. Abraham asked God if He would also destroy the righteous in those cities.

Who would argue with God? And who would expect to change His mind? No one, right?

Well, Moses did. When God grew frustrated with the Israelites' disobedience and was ready to call it quits, Moses talked Him into giving them one more chance. Abraham did it again when God was set on destroying two whole cities. Abraham tried to talk God out of His plan for the sake of any righteous souls that might reside there. Because of Abraham's pleas, Lot and his family were saved from the destruction.

Both these incidences demonstrate two very

important things about the nature of God—the first being that God prefers an honest relationship over blind obedience. And the second is that God is merciful and just. He truly listens to the desires of our hearts and wants us to contribute to His divine plan!

Son of Man

For the Son of man is come to save that which was lost.
MATTHEW 18:11 KJV

- Name of God the Son

- Jesus is referred to as the "Son of man" eighty-eight times in the KJV.

- The words *Son of Man* are usually translated from terms meaning "Son of Adam" or "Son of Enosh." The first interpretation is seen as a direct link to God, while the second is often seen as a link to the generation where mankind separated itself from God by turning to idolatry.

- Jesus explains that the good shepherd would not be content with saving ninety-nine out of a hundred sheep but would brave the storm to find one lost lamb. He sees each of us as that one lamb worth saving.

The expression "Son of man" is used in different ways in the Bible. Jesus used the simplest interpretation. There was no artful pretense, no deep meaning, He simply meant "I am one of you." The love and humility in Jesus' statement is enough to make being an ordinary man or woman something worth aspiring to—and enough to make the Son of Man someone well worth adoring!

Dayspring

Through the tender mercy of our God; whereby the dayspring from on high hath visited us, To give light to them that sit in darkness and in the shadow of death, to guide our feet into the way of peace.
LUKE 1:78–79 KJV

- Name of God the Son

- Jesus is called "dayspring" once in the KJV.

- *Dayspring* means "the breaking of the dawn." It was a common term in England when the King James Bible was being compiled.

- The birth of his son was a wonderful time for Zechariah—so wonderful that he composed a song of praise for God. But instead of singing about his son, he thanked God for the child he knew was already on the way, the Dayspring.

The dayspring is the point on the horizon where the sun first appears. Of course that point changes as the seasons progress. Every day the sun rises is a slightly different place. That place can be tracked and predicted—but the appearance of the Son in our lives rarely happens when we expect it. One thing is for sure though, whenever and wherever the Dayspring occurs in our lives, everything changes!

Scripture Index

Genesis
3:15 75
15:2 37
16:13 130
18:25 149
22:14 62
49:10 44

Exodus
3:14 7
15:26 146
16:31 104

Numbers
11:25 144
24:17 50

Deuteronomy
32:4 29

Judges
6:23–24 139

2 Samuel
22:47 113

Job
4:17 94
9:33 134
33:4 34

Psalms
5:12 96
18:13 42
18:30 111
23:3 77
72:6 53
83:18 17
90:1 78
121:5 95

Proverbs
18:10 39

Song of Solomon
2:1 9

Isaiah
9:6 . . . . 24, 43
25:4 127
28:5 61
42:6 119
53:11 115
64:8 21

Jeremiah
2:13 70
8:22 26
10:16 125
31:31–32 101

Ezekiel
34:29 84

Daniel
6:20 138
7:9 10

Haggai
2:7 129

Zechariah
2:5 86
3:8 54
8:22 47

Malachi
3:2 . . . . 92, 124

Matthew
1:21 107
1:23 76
9:15 19
9:38 117
11:19 56
16:16 109
18:11 151

Mark
6:3 33
10:45 45
14:36 51

Luke
1:35 90
1:68–69 99
1:78–79 152
5:30–31 67

John
1:1 142
1:29 27
1:41 40
1:45 89
1:49 31
3:2 41
4:10 97
6:35, 48 35
8:12 66
10:9 136
10:11 15
14:6 73
15:1 12

Acts
20:28 13

Romans
8:15 49

1 Corinthians
5:7 59
15:23 82
15:45 . . . . 87, 141

2 Corinthians

  1:3 . . . . 57, 122

Ephesians

  2:19–20 64

1 Timothy

  6:15 148

Hebrews

  1:3 79

  2:10 135

  3:1 69

  6:20 121

  9:14 72

  12:2 80

  12:28–29 46

James

  1:17 103

1 Peter

  2:4 71

  4:14 132

1 John

  2:1 105

Revelation

  3:14 48

  19:16 88

  22:13 23

  22:16 98

Name Index

Abba 51

Adonai. 37

Advocate 105

Alpha and Omega. 23

Amen. 48

Ancient of Days 10

Author and Finisher of
    Our Faith. 80

Balm of Gilead 26

Branch, The 54

Bread of Life. 35

Breath of the Almighty . .34

Bridegroom 19

Buckler 111

Captain of Their
    Salvation 135

Carpenter 33

Chief Cornerstone 64

Christ, The 109

Consuming Fire. 46

Covenant of the
    People 119

Daysman 134

Dayspring 152

Desire of All Nations . . . 129

Diadem of Beauty. 61

Door, The 136

Dwelling Place. 78

El-Elyon. 42

Emmanuel. 76

Eternal Spirit. 72

Father of Lights. 103

Father of Mercies 122

Firstfruits 82

Forerunner. 121

Fountain of Living
    Waters 70

Friend of Sinners 56

Fullers' Soap 124

Gift of God 97

God of All Comfort 57

God Who Sees 130

Good Shepherd. 15

High Priest 69

Holy Ghost 13

Horn of Salvation. 99

Husband 101

I Am 7

Jehovah 17

Jehovahjireh 62

Jehovahshalom 139

Jesus. 107

Jesus of Nazareth 89

Judge of All the Earth . . 149

King of Israel 31

King of Kings 88

Lamb of God 27

Last Adam. 141

Light of the World 66

Living God 138

Living Stone 71

Lord of Hosts 47

Lord of the Harvest . . . 117

Lord Who Heals 146

Majesty on High 79

Maker 94

Manna. 104

Messiah 40

Morning Star 98

Passover Lamb 59

Physician 67

Plant of Renown 84

Portion. 125

Potentate 148

Potter. 21

Power of the Highest . . . 90

Prince of Peace 43

Quickening Spirit 87

Rabbi. 41

Rain upon Mown

   Grass 53

Ransom. 45

Refiner's Fire. 92

Refuge. 127

Restorer. 77

Righteous Servant. 115

Rock, The 29

Rose of Sharon, The. 9

Savior 113

Seed of the Woman 75

Shade. 95

Shield 96

Shiloh 44

Spirit of Adoption. 49

Spirit of Glory. 132

Spirit That Was upon

   Moses. 144

Star out of Jacob 50

Strong Tower. 39

Son of Man. 151

Vine. 12

Wall of Fire 86

Way, The 73

Wonderful Counselor . . . 24

Word, The. 142